# THE ABCS OF SCHOOL
# SUCCESS

# THE ABCs OF SCHOOL
# SUCCESS

Tips, Checklists, and Strategies
for Equipping Your Child

## WESLEY SHARPE, EdD

a division of Baker Publishing Group
Grand Rapids, Michigan

© 2008 by Wesley Sharpe

Published by Revell
a division of Baker Publishing Group
P.O. Box 6287, Grand Rapids, MI 49516-6287
www.revellbooks.com

Printed in the United States of America

Library of Congress Cataloging-in-Publication Data
Sharpe, Wesley, 1928–
    The ABCs of school success : tips, checklists, and strategies for equipping
your child / Wesley Sharpe.
        p.  cm.
    Includes bibliographical references.
    ISBN 978-0-8007-3226-4 (pbk.)
    1. Education—Parent participation. 2. Home and school. I. Title.
LB1048.5.S53 2008
371.19'2—dc22                                              2008012981

# Contents

7

# Contents

# Contents

# Introduction

I love the first day of school. I enjoy watching excited, bright-eyed children eager to meet their new teachers and old friends. Most kids love learning. They are happy to be in school in spite of their grumbling about the end of summer vacation and the beginning of homework. But for some children, the magic of school ends abruptly.

By about the middle of the school year, children who aren't learning to read or can't understand simple math concepts are referred by their teachers for testing. And other issues can block school success. Research shows that many children begin to hide their natural creativity at about the fourth grade as they struggle with rigid assignments and rote learning.

I've written this book for moms and dads. It's a book for busy parents, not the kind of book you need to read from cover to cover. Instead, keep it handy; dive in and find the information you need. Or begin with the final chapter and skim through the chapter summaries. Then locate the chapter you want to read and absorb the in-depth information for that topic.

*The ABCs of School Success* reflects solid, up-to-date psychological and educational research. Lists, quizzes, and sidebars give you quick access to information that will guide you in helping your children achieve their full potential in school. Use this book as a comprehensive, success-oriented reference book that takes some of the mystery out of helping your children learn.

# 1

# Make Learning Fun

When I think back to the birth of our first child, I realize how little we knew about our son's early development. Of course, that was fifty years ago, and I doubt I would have guessed he was taking speech and language lessons before he was born.

Now we know that the infant's brain is vastly more complex than previously thought. Current research indicates that unborn babies hear and respond to familiar voices. And soon after babies are born, many can tell the difference between their native language and other languages. In other words, learning has already taken place in the womb. "Newborns apparently learn the rhythm of their native language and of their mother's voice while in the womb," says Peter Jusczyk, professor of psychology at Johns Hopkins University.[1]

Children need to be touched, to be spoken to, and to have the opportunity to explore and experiment. Recent advances in brain research give us some explanations. For example, from birth on, an infant's brain requires almost nonstop stimulation. And evidence is mounting that what you say to your baby and the way you say it will give a boost to her speech and language development.

The American Academy of Pediatrics recommends that infants be exposed to no television in the first two years of life. An AAP study published in May 2007 said that about 70 percent of children under the age of two watch some television starting at about nine months. Furthermore, 20 percent of two-year-olds have television sets in their rooms.

According to Dr. Dimitri Christakis, "The best available evidence to date suggests that certainly watching a lot of TV before the age of two is in fact harmful—harmful in terms of children's attentional abilities later in life, harmful in terms of their cognitive development, both of those measured at school entry."[2]

### Help Young Children Learn to Solve Problems

Children must solve problems each day. These problems range from simple ones ("What socks should I wear to school today?") to serious ones ("I am afraid of the boy who hits me!"). Even small children can learn to problem solve if the problems are kept at a simple level.

#### 5 Suggestions for Teaching Tiny Tots to Problem Solve

1. Don't ask yes or no questions; keep them open ended.
2. See how many answers can be generated in a few minutes.
3. Don't worry if the answers are outlandish or unrealistic.
4. Encourage unconventional uses of ordinary things. For instance, a pillow could be a stool.
5. Make up a simple story with a problem and talk about ways to solve the problem.

"Choose high-quality literature to get started. Try pairing a book of fiction with a nonfiction book on the same topic. This makes for an unbeatable combination that will have your child begging for more books to read on his or her own—and with a partner. When parents ask me what they can do to improve their fourth grader's or older child's reading skills, they are often surprised at the simplicity of my answer. 'Please read to your child and have him or her read to you.' While many of us read aloud to very young children, some may abandon the practice as youngsters reach third or fourth grade and begin to read independently. But children up to any age can benefit tremendously from shared reading sessions," said Mary Rose, a fourth grade teacher at Lake Sybelia Elementary School in Maitland, Florida.[3]

## Have Fun Reading Aloud

Do your kids fuss if you forget to read a bedtime story? Even if they fall asleep reading, don't worry about it, because the benefits of reading aloud are worth the effort. Reading a story is more than a way to get your kids to quiet down before bedtime.

Reading aloud is one of the most important parenting activities you can perform. "The single variable that's been found in repeated studies as having an impact on children's school success—not just learning to read—is the number of stories they have had read to them before they come to school," said Dr. Jane Braunger, a senior research associate with the Strategic Literacy Initiative in Oakland, California.[4]

### Reasons to Read Aloud to Young Children

1. Daily read-aloud sessions promote language development in young children.
2. Children who are read to learn to read more easily.
3. Reading aloud increases your child's vocabulary.
4. Reading aloud is a way to boost your child's school achievement.
5. Reading aloud expands your child's imagination and stimulates curiosity and creativity.
6. Children who are read to begin to make the connection between reading and writing.
7. Reading promotes values and higher-level thinking.

### Reasons to Read Aloud to Older Children

1. Reading aloud increases the older child's enjoyment of books.
2. Reading aloud makes difficult books more interesting and easier to understand.
3. Reading aloud helps children learn how what they read relates to life.
4. Reading aloud helps children check for missed, skipped, and mispronounced words.
5. Reading aloud helps kids enjoy the excitement of the unfolding story.

### 6 Ways to Explore Books with Young Children

1. Make a reading place.
2. Visit the library.
3. Buy board books.
4. Buy books the child can touch and explore.
5. Encourage the child to participate.
6. Get silly. Be an actor.[5]

## 7 Read-Aloud Do's and Don'ts

1. Do become familiar with a large quantity of books on topics that interest your child. Be certain your child is exposed to high-quality literature.
2. Do preview the book. Will your child understand the book's concepts and vocabulary?
3. Do show the illustrations to your child, and stop reading once in a while to answer questions. Give the child enough time to study the illustrations.
4. Don't read stories you hate. Your dislike of a book will seep through to your child and might turn her off to reading.
5. Don't choose books that will overwhelm your child. Select read-alouds that will entertain and teach ideas at his intellectual, emotional, and developmental level.
6. Don't answer questions that stop the story's flow or give away its plot. Let the suspense build as your child anticipates the ending.
7. If he or she gets too wiggly, take a break or end the session with a good-night kiss. Five or ten minutes may be all she can take at one reading. If it happens regularly, ask yourself, "Is this book the right level for my child?"[6]

## Books That Count

If there's one school subject that children complain about most, it's math. Here's the good news: new studies report that kids can eliminate their fears and nurture their math quotient by reading books that integrate simple math into the story line.

Reading out loud is a way to jump-start your grade school child's mathematical thinking and help eliminate the math doldrums. Even children who can't read yet can benefit when their parents read fun and interesting material.

## 10 Math Stories That Kids Love

These storybooks help children discover how math comes in handy in everyday life.

1. *Riddle-Iculous Math* by Joan Holub (Albert Whitman & Company, 2003). Kids will love the stories about the Egg and Spoon Race and will meet the Spud Brothers and other characters while learning addition, subtraction, and fractions.
2. *Sir Cumference and the Great Knight of Angleland* by Cindy Neuschwander (Charlesbridge Publishing, 2001). Sir Cumference's son, Radius, will earn his knighthood if he rescues a king. The circular medallion (a protractor) given to Radius by his father and his mother, Lady Di of Ameter, helps him examine every angle along the way.
3. *Monster Money* by Grace Maccarone and Marilyn Burns (Cartwheel Books, 1998). Ten smiling monsters make a trip to a pet store to buy a pet. Children learn to recognize and count different combinations of pennies, nickels, and dimes.
4. *Amanda Bean's Amazing Dream* by Cindy Neuschwander and Marilyn Burns (Scholastic Press, 1998). Amanda Bean counts everything from books in the library to popcorn in her bowl, but she discovers she can count faster if she learns to multiply.
5. *Even Steven and Odd Todd* by Kathryn Cristaldi (Cartwheel Books, 1996). Children learn basic number concepts in the story of a mismatched pair of cousins with different number preferences.
6. *How Big Is a Foot?* by Rolf Myller (Dell, 1999). How big should the queen's new bed be? No one knows! In this book, children learn about measurement.
7. *How Much Is a Million?* by David M. Schwartz (Scholastic Press, 1993). To count to a million will take you about twenty-three days.

8. *One Hundred Hungry Ants* by Elinor J. Pinczes (Houghton Mifflin, 1999). An introduction to math that youngsters will enjoy. In this whimsical story kids learn the everyday math necessary to make change for a dollar.
9. *Anno's Mysterious Multiplying Jar* by Masaichiro Anno and Mitsumasa Anno (Putnam Publishing Group, 1999). A story about what is in one magic jar. An easy-to-read book that moves from concrete to abstract math concepts with riddles like "If there are three kingdoms in two countries on one island, then how many kingdoms are there altogether?"
10. *Counting on Frank* by Rod Clement (Garth Stevens Publishing, 1991). A boy loves to ask questions about ordinary things: his father and the bathtub, humpback whales, peas. And he uses his dog Frank as a unit of measurement. Together they present counting, size comparison, and mathematical facts.

## 4 Strategies for Making the Most of Math-Related Stories

1. Examine the book's cover and title for hints about the story's theme.
2. If your child can read, read the book to him, and then ask him to read it out loud.
3. Refer back to what your child knows about the characters and help her to recall other information.
4. Discuss new math words such as add, subtract, multiply, and divide, and post them on the fridge or bulletin board.

## 4 Websites to Refresh Your Child's Math Skills

Math skills are vulnerable to breaks in your child's schedule that take him away from his daily math lessons. And it's easy for math skills to melt away during the summer break. If you have ever tried to get your child to concentrate on math problems while his buddies are having fun outside, you know the problem. However, you may find the answer to math boredom online. The following websites will help kids retain their math skills, exercise their minds, and have fun too.

1. Middle-grade math students will love the animated story found at Villainy, Inc. Children sign on as agents of the AVU (Anti-Villainy Unit) and try to thwart the wicked Dr. Wick. Agents pretend to go along with Wick and use their math skills to help him succeed. The activities at this site explore statistics and probability, algebra, geometry, decimals, percentages, and more. "Each story offers tongue-in-cheek dialogue along with comical animated characters and scenes that set the stage for mathematical success." Get started at http://villainyinc.thinkport.org/story/default.asp.

2. *Batter's Up Baseball* is a game of addition and multiplication baseball found at http://www.prongo.com/math/. It allows players to select a single (easy), double (harder), or home run (hardest) math problem. After players select the pitcher's challenge, a screen will come up with a math problem. A correct answer moves players around the bases. Get it wrong, and it's a strike. As everyone knows, three strikes and you're out. This is a fun game for kids who need to practice math basics.

3. How often does your child ask, "Why do I have to know this?" The site http://www.learner.org/exhibits/dailymath/ explains how math helps us make decisions about our lives. And it gives eye-opening answers to questions about gambling, credit cards, tasty recipes, and more.

4. Why not let your children make their own math worksheets for free with the help of the Math Worksheet Creator (http://www.superkids.com/aweb/tools/math/)? Kids can select a variety of operations including addition and subtraction, multiplication, division, fractions, percentages, and more. Kids choose the minimum and maximum numbers to be used in the problems and click on the button to print their customized worksheet.

## Award-Winning Websites

The Internet offers nearly unlimited opportunities for fun, creativity, and learning. The following websites were chosen for their wholesome, lively, and exhilarating approach to learning and fun. Many experts advise parents that kids should access the Web only when an adult is present to supervise. With that in mind, whether your child is just learning to navigate the Internet or already surfs like a pro, these family-friendly websites will provide hours of fun and learning.

1. Storyplace.org is a digital library for children. The interactive format and easy point-and-click navigation make this a site young children will enjoy. Children learn beginning reading, counting, and coloring skills.
2. A good site for elementary grades and up is http://yucky.kids.discovery.com. "The yuckiest site on the Internet" teaches earth science and human biology. It uses children's love of the disgusting to explore the living sciences.
3. Gigglepoetry.com is an award-winning, humorous site that makes writing poetry fun. Children in grades three to eight can take classes, enter contests, and read winning poetry written by kids. Children learn how to write nursery rhymes, limericks, and more.
4. Clubhousemagazine.org is the online edition of Focus on the Family's *Clubhouse* magazine. This site has variety to spare for elementary-aged kids. Does your child thrive on humor? Then the Jokes section will keep her in stitches. And Fun Stuff includes puzzles, crafts, recipes, and kids' art.
5. Also from Focus on the Family, check out Whit's End, the official *Adventures in Odyssey* radio show website, at http://www.whitsend.org/.
6. At www.kids-space.org, children write and read stories written by other kids or listen to music composed by children.

21

Kids' Space is a site for elementary and middle school children.

7. Snoopy.com is the official "Peanuts" website. Each day the home page features a different comic strip by the late Charles M. Schulz. Kids will enjoy browsing through the strip archive, viewing movies, or visiting the game gallery.

8. PBS Kids (http://pbskids.org) is the online site where children can interact with their favorite characters from PBS television shows. Geared for kids aged two to twelve, the site offers various levels of interactivity. PBS Kids also encourages offline activities and gives suggestions for creative play.

9. Find links to about one hundred Christian and other wholesome sites on the Internet at http://netministries.org/kids.htmls.

10. With 35 million page views per month, FunBrain.com may be the number one site for children. It is filled with educational games for kids in kindergarten through eighth grade. Games are categorized and given enticing titles such as Fresh Baked Fractions, Translator Alligator, and Proton Don.

11. A combination of fun and exceptional content and design make Funology.com an award-winning site. The site is filled with games, riddles, puzzles, science experiments, and magic tricks. Each craft project, experiment, or magic trick includes a list of things necessary to complete the task.

12. The site http://www.mamamedia.com offers nearly one hundred activities, plus opportunities to view other kids' material and post their own. The site emphasizes creative thinking, logic, reading, writing, communication skills, and self-expression.

13. Nickelodeon (http://www.nick.com) is a site for all children. Since boredom isn't part of the program, there is never a dull moment. Kids can visit their favorite Nickelodeon television characters and check out daily specials, games,

pictures, and more. Daily and weekly changes make this a high-interest site.

14. National Geographic Kids (http://kids.nationalgeographic .com) is filled with material written for kids. The mix of fun and fact make it a site well worth visiting. For instance, children who visit the Cartoon Factory learn to write the dialogue for a cartoon. On the serious side, the Bookworm Corner gives children the chance to tell about their favorite books.

15. The Smithsonian Zoo's "Just for Kids" section (http://nationalzoo.si.edu/Audiences/kids) is loaded with fascinating pictures and information about twenty-two of the zoo's birds and animals. Children can solve jigsaw puzzles and crossword puzzles, take a virtual world tour, and learn about animals and their names. This is a site for children's enjoyment, and it gives homework help too.

16. Bonus.com features hundreds of games, puzzles, and activities that invite children to play, imagine, explore, color, and find new fun. The site was developed as a free, one-stop center for entertainment. Internet safety is a top priority.

17. Thunk.com provides safe, educational, Web-based fun. Kids learn about secret codes and can send secret messages to their friends.

## Wanted! Grandpa and Grandma

Does your child need help with her academics? Or does he need someone to sound off to about school? Most children think their grandparents are cool, and the influence of a grandpa or grandma is remarkable. Cool grandparents are gentle teachers of the way life should be. While they read aloud to your child or explain a math concept, they also will pass on a little of what they know about life.

The apostle Paul makes clear the powerful effect of grandparents on their grandchildren. He wrote to Timothy, "I have been reminded of your sincere faith, which first lived in your grandmother Lois and in your mother Eunice and, I am persuaded, lives in you also" (2 Tim. 1:5).

What's the payoff? For grandparents it is the unique bond they will develop with their grandchild. For the grandchild it's associating with a grandparent who loves him unconditionally, who listens to his tale of woe about school, and who helps him academically. Like Timothy's grandmother, grandparents touch the lives and faith of their grandchildren.

### 4 Tips for Getting Grandparents Involved

1. Make a pact with your children's grandparents. A good parent-grandparent agreement on discipline goes like this: grandparents handle minor discipline problems, but mom or dad takes care of any serious breach of rules. When kids understand this, discipline is easier.
2. Encourage trips to the library. Preschool story times and puppet shows make the library a fascinating place for youngsters. Older children like to explore the bookshelves. Ask your child's grandparent to help her check out books or magazines that appeal to her interests.
3. Ask grandparents to put together a supply of art materials. Start with colored marking pens, watercolor paints, and art paper. Cutting out magazine pictures, using paste, and painting with watercolors are messy activities, so be sure to designate a place for the children to work away from valuable furniture or carpets.
4. Encourage grandparents to invite hard questions and listen to their grandchild's opinions. Insist that no question is too dumb to ask. Sometimes an important conversation will begin with a tug on grandma's sleeve and "Hey, Grandma, you know what?"

# 2

# Growing Up Smart

A favorite book of my children was a worn-out, dog-eared volume of Bible stories. The kids always listened attentively when I read one of the stories. They never seemed to grow tired of them, and we read some stories over and over.

A good story is one that children can touch and feel with their imaginations. When children travel on imaginary flights, they use the mysterious and artistic side of their brain where feelings, emotions, dreams, and creativity are born.

God created us with a brain that functions in emotional and creative ways. The logical side of the brain is in control when children learn story facts, but when they go beyond factual information, they are beginning to think creatively.

## Left- and Right-Brain Learning

To accomplish balanced thinking, the brain is divided into left and right hemispheres. Preferences are developed early, and as children find success with one side of their brain, it becomes more dominant. For instance, the child who is better at art than reading may develop a preference for art and neglect reading.

Children can learn to develop the skills of the less-preferred side. Many children make the shift from left- to right-brained thinking. Others become stuck in one hemisphere or the other and end up using the wrong side of the brain for the thinking they need to do.

### 11 Facts about Left-Brain Dominant Children

1. They remember through language.
2. They read for details and facts.
3. They learn through systematic plans.
4. They process information sequentially.
5. They are happy when winning.
6. They recognize and remember names.
7. They thrive on well-structured assignments.
8. They use logic to solve problems.
9. They enjoy realistic stories.
10. They respond to verbal instructions.
11. They think independently.

### 11 Facts about Right-Brain Dominant Children

1. They remember images and pictures.
2. They read for main ideas.
3. They learn through exploration.
4. They process information in patterns.
5. They believe sports are for fun.
6. They recognize and remember faces.
7. They work best on open-ended assignments.
8. They use intuition to solve problems.
9. They enjoy fantasy, poetry, or myths.
10. They respond to visual/kinesthetic instruction.
11. They are sensitive.

## Find Your Child's Preference

| My child's right-brain qualities: | My child's left-brain qualities: |
|---|---|
| _____ | _____ |
| _____ | _____ |
| _____ | _____ |
| _____ | _____ |

## Brainstorming for Problem Solving

Brainstorming is a right-brain problem-solving method that has everyday applications for your family: completing homework, settling arguments, planning vacations, and cleaning rooms. When children discover that they won't be criticized for expressing silly ideas, they feel better about themselves, and their improved self-esteem generates new confidence in their abilities.

### 4 Brainstorming Rules

1. Free your imagination.
2. Wait to judge the ideas.
3. The more ideas the better.
4. Combine your ideas to make them better.

### 6 Important Points to Remember about Brainstorming

1. Brainstorming teaches youngsters to play with ideas and to produce a large number of ideas leading to the solution of a problem.
2. No idea is bad.
3. The basic strategy is to delay judging the merit of ideas until all ideas have been listed.
4. Prejudging ideas restricts the flow of good ideas.
5. Family members are free to use their intuition and to be flexible in their thinking.

6. Brainstorming is a right-brain activity; the left brain comes into play later during the evaluation of the ideas and the selection of the best ones.

## A Checklist of Discovery Questions

Alex Osborn has developed a number of questions that may be used in brainstorming to stretch and expand creative thinking. A summary of these ideas follows:

1. What new use can I put this to?
2. How can I adapt the idea to another use?
3. How can I modify the idea? For instance, could I change the meaning, color, motion, sound, odor, form, or shape? How can I give it a new twist?
4. How could I expand the idea? Could I add something to make it stronger, higher, longer, etc.?

### An Example of Creative Imagination

Several years ago the children in the third grade in Moraga, California, were required to invent something original, and the kids came up with some beauties. One crop of inventions included a water-saving device that shuts off the shower, ready or not; a battery-run back-scratcher for pets; and a basketball launcher for little kids whose shots fall short of the basket.

One boy invented an elaborate security system to keep roaming dogs and cats off his front lawn. It used motion sensors and automatic timers to set off sprinklers, plus a tape recording of a roaring lion. The only problem was that his system couldn't tell the difference between a wandering dog and the next-door neighbor coming to visit.

5. Could I streamline the idea by omitting, shortening, or subtracting something from it?
6. Could I reverse or combine it with something else? Turn it around? Turn it upside down or inside out?[1]

## Homework: Good or Bad?

Why is homework so important anyway? You may not be able to convince your kids that it is, but educators agree that homework increases a child's learning as long as it isn't simply busywork and it is kept within reasonable boundaries. The length of time homework should take depends on your child's grade level and the teacher's requirements. However, the U.S. Department of Education recommends that homework be limited to 10 to 20 minutes a day for grades kindergarten to second grade and 30 to 60 minutes for grades three to six. Assignments will vary for grades seven to nine, but homework generally takes longer once kids have multiple teachers.

### Key Strategies for Homework

1. Set up a homework center that gives the child the feeling that it is a place for work. If possible, get away from the noise of the family hubbub. If your child needs to be near you to stay on task, try the kitchen or dining room table.
2. Outfit the center with a kid-sized desk and supplies such as pencils, pens, colored markers, a dictionary, and a thesaurus.
3. Depending on the age of your child, you may also wish to include a computer or laptop.
4. If possible, install a bulletin board to post long-term assignments and other important dates.
5. To get your child in the homework habit, try to schedule homework time at the same time every day.
6. Set up a daily schedule with your child. Together estimate how long it will take to finish each subject's assignment. Use a daily homework planner.

7. Remember that breaks refresh your child, especially if she is in the lower grades. But older children also need an occasional break because of their longer assignments.

## The Value of Journaling

Journaling promotes both right- and left-brain functioning. If your child is stressed out by school or other events in his personal life, keeping a journal may be the best way he can reduce his stress. Children's lives are loaded with stress. Moving to a new school or neighborhood, a change in their class schedule, or a new acquaintance often contributes to their stress.

Encouraging journaling is a way to influence and aid your child's thinking and emotional development. Keeping a journal encourages thinking and communicating, stimulates creativity, and promotes emotional awareness and imagination.

### Benefits of Journaling

1. Journal writing eliminates the pressure to perform. A basic rule: no one looks at my child's journal unless they have his or her permission.
2. Journal keeping influences right-brain and left-brain development and helps establish balanced thinking.
3. The combination of art and writing stimulates both visual thinking (right brain) and logical thinking (left brain). Writing enhances the child's logical left-brain thinking, while the drawing and artwork stimulate right-brain, nonverbal thinking and imagination.
4. Before a child begins a class assignment, writes a letter, or makes a decision, she can write her thoughts in her journal. The child develops her own thinking and states her opinions honestly.

30

## Journaling Tips

1. Have notebooks and writing and drawing supplies ready.
2. Assign a topic to get your child started.
3. Ask your child what he would like to write about.

## 8 Topics for the Journal Writer

1. Draw a picture of your family having fun together.
2. Write and illustrate a scene from your favorite book.
3. Write about your favorite holiday.
4. Draw a picture or write about how you feel when you're angry.
5. Imagine you're a character in a Bible story. Tell what you like and don't like about where you live.
6. Write about what makes you happy or sad.
7. Interview one of your grandparents and find out about your family history.
8. Imagine you are in your favorite spot. Draw a picture or write about it.

## Help Your Daughter Succeed

Elisabeth's personality sparkled and snapped. As a curious, confident, and independent fifth grader, she was a straight-A student with a passion for math and science. Her career goal was to become a pediatrician. But junior high school was a different story. Her grades dipped until she was barely hanging on. In the ninth grade she announced a new goal to her mom. "I'm going to be a cosmetologist," she said. "I stink at math. It's too hard, and I'm just not good enough."

Something is wrong with this picture. As a school psychologist, I know that boys and girls start out on an equal footing. The difference between their average IQ scores is insignificant. In fact, some experts believe girls are more mature and ready to learn. Still, by the time girls graduate from high school, their excitement has ebbed.

What happens to the bright-eyed exuberance of girls between the primary grades and high school graduation? Although boys and girls start school on an equal footing, different expectations for girls and boys show up early in a child's school career. For example, the teacher may call on boys to respond to questions more often than girls, some teachers value boys' comments more than girls, or classroom seating arrangements may favor boys.

Here are some ways to improve your daughter's achievement, build her confidence and self-esteem, and overcome gender bias.

### 10 Ways to Promote Fairness in Your Daughter's Education

1. Focus on good education. Different expectations for girls and boys show up early in a child's school career.
2. Visit the classroom often, and if possible, make a video recording of the classroom activities.
3. Check with her teacher. Be certain your daughter has equal access to hands-on experience with computers, lab equipment, and tools.
4. Be positive and nonconfrontational when you suggest changes to the teacher.
5. Find out if your daughter is experiencing excessive teasing by boys. Ask her, "What do boys say when they tease you?"
6. Assure your daughter that intelligence and good grades are an asset. Preteen and teenage girls often are swayed by the opinions of other kids.
7. Encourage her abilities and recognize her accomplishments.

## One Girl's Opinion

"In the sixth grade I got to attend a meeting with female scientists and engineers. We got to meet a lot of people who actually do science. Before, when I thought of a scientist, I thought of a mad scientist with weird hair and a lot of vials. Now I know that isn't true."

Jane, age twelve

8. Help her to develop qualities like independence, courage, honesty, and creativity.
9. Pay attention to the movies she watches and the books she reads. Do they stereotype women or leave them out entirely?
10. Watch out for put-downs. Don't allow family members to make demeaning remarks about your daughter.

## Guy-ifying School for Boys

While the effort to improve the academic achievement of girls has been successful, some experts believe that schools are now failing boys. You probably wouldn't be surprised to hear that your son behaves differently than girls, and sometimes his behavior gets him into big trouble.

Dr. William Pollack, who is a Harvard Medical School psychologist, director for the Center for Men and Young Men at Harvard Medical School's McLean Hospital, and author of *Real Boys: Rescuing our Sons from the Myths of Boyhood*, believes that boys have a unique learning style. Furthermore, by engaging in some action-oriented tasks, schools can help boys boost their academic performance and improve their self-esteem. Research suggests that while many girls may prefer to learn by watching or listening, boys

generally prefer to learn by doing, says Pollack. By design-
ing an inviting educational experience for boys and "guy-
ifying" certain aspects of schools, we can help boys thrive
as individuals.[2]

## Single-Gender Schools and Classes

In the last decade the number of public schools switching
to single-gender instruction and single-gender classes has
jumped from approximately 5 to 240 schools. While this is
only a small fraction of the 93,000 public schools nationwide,
experts say that in the future, we will see a proliferation of
single-sex schools.

With a boost from the 2001 No Child Left Behind Act,
federal money allocated to schools for innovative programs
may be used for all-boys' and all-girls' schools and classes.
The result is an increased interest in single-sex schools
because they appear to be a way to overcome the "boy
crisis."

### Some Myths and Facts about Single-Gender Learning

**Myth:** Boys and girls need to be in separate classes because they learn at different speeds.

**Fact:** Boys and girls learn better in separate classes, but
it's not because boys are smarter than girls or girls are way
ahead of boys intellectually. Rather, they simply learn in
different ways.

**Myth:** Girls use both sides of the brain more symmetri-
cally than boys, which explains their ability to complete
multiple tasks and tune in to emotions.

**Fact:** While there are essentially no differences between
the intelligence test scores of men and women, they do use
different brain areas to achieve similar IQ results. University
of California at Irvine research findings suggest that men

tend to excel in tasks like mathematics while women tend to excel in language facility.[3]

**Myth:** Boys focus on objects and are biologically programmed for math and science, while girls focus on relationships.

**Fact:** This idea is false. It was based on a poorly constructed research study using day-old babies.

### 7 Points about the Learning Styles of Boys and Girls

1. Boys often sit in the back of the classroom where they can't hear the teacher. Girls who sit at the front think the teacher is yelling at them. This difference can be corrected by switching the seating arrangement.
2. Sitting in a circle or in small groups is distracting in co-ed classes, although it is a good arrangement in single-sex classes.
3. Girls tend to have higher academic standards than boys.
4. Girls examine their performance more critically than boys.
5. School grade comparisons show that girls outperform boys at all age levels.
6. Girls who make straight A's often think they are stupid, and boys with B grades believe they are brilliant. Girls need to be encouraged, and boys need a reality check.
7. Small group learning works well for girls.

### A Visit to a Single-Gender Class

Classes at Lyseth Elementary School in Portland, Maine, were involved in a two-year study to see if fourth-grade boys and girls learn better in all-girls' and all-boys' classrooms. The half-day school program was the first of its kind in the Maine public school system. It attempted to raise boys' lagging reading and writing scores by providing single-sex classes to accommodate boys' and girls' different learning styles. The students' progress will be tracked through middle school to check the long-term effects of the program. What did the boys say about their classroom? A nine-year-old boy said, "It seems calmer without the girls." "If we have a boy teacher, we can learn better," said another. And some boys reported that their class helped them open up with each other because it was just for boys.

### 7 Reasons Why a Single-Gender Class Helps Boys

1. Often boys are classified as having behavior problems without considering their emotional needs.
2. Boys' reading and writing problems often go unnoticed.
3. Boys associate reading with feminine skills.
4. Boys prefer learning by doing. They like action-oriented classes.
5. Educators and parents fail to take into account boys' high energy levels and unique learning styles.
6. A single-gender class can make a difference emotionally and academically for boys.
7. Single-gender classes improve academic performance, improve motivation to study, and reduce clowning around and other distracting behaviors boys use to impress girls.

### Behavior Checklist for Boys

Use this behavior checklist to evaluate your son's behavior. The following behaviors are characteristic of boys who improve in a single-gender class.

| Behavior | Yes | No |
|---|---|---|
| Acts out at school | ___ | ___ |
| Has a high energy level | ___ | ___ |
| Doesn't like reading | ___ | ___ |
| Believes reading is for girls | ___ | ___ |
| Has low reading and writing scores | ___ | ___ |

| | | |
|---|---|---|
| Doesn't like school | ___ | ___ |
| Has low educational expectations | ___ | ___ |
| Lacks interest in his classes | ___ | ___ |

Reasons why my son probably would benefit from a single-gender class:

1. _____

2. _____

3. _____

4. _____

## Dads Make a Difference

Dads sometimes find it difficult to take on multiple roles that include participating in classroom activities, school meetings, and events. But experts say children whose fathers participate in classroom activities and school meetings and events receive higher grades, enjoy school more, and are more likely to participate in extracurricular activities.

### 5 Ways Dad Can Make a Difference

1. Get involved in your child's classroom and school activities.
2. Go beyond the traditional back-to-school night and parent-teacher conferences.
3. Visit your child's classroom and offer to tutor kids who need special help.
4. Suggest an annual coffee and donut day in the school cafeteria, and invite fathers and significant men in the children's lives.

5. Interview your child and ask questions like:
   a. Who is your favorite teacher?
   b. What do you like most about school?
   c. Who is your best friend?
   d. What do you think I do for a living?
   e. Where would you like to go on vacation this year?

# 3

# Learning and Creativity

Have you heard of the marshmallow test? It was not a test to improve the flavor of marshmallows but a serious research study to measure the ability of kids to resist their impulse for immediate gratification in pursuit of a long-range goal. Daniel Goleman describes the experiment in his book *Emotional Intelligence: Why It Can Matter More Than IQ*.[1]

In the 1960s a group of four-year olds were subjects in a study conducted by psychologist Walter Mischel at Stanford University. He made this proposal to a group of children at a preschool on the university campus: "I am leaving for a few minutes to run an errand. If you will wait until I return, you can have two marshmallows for a treat when I return. If you can't wait until then, you can have only one—but you can have it right now."

While about one third of the children grabbed the marshmallow immediately, some children waited a little longer, and one third waited fifteen or twenty minutes for the researcher to return.

"When the researchers tracked down the children fourteen years later, they found that this test was an amazing predictor of how they did in school. The kids who waited were more emotionally stable, better liked by their teachers and peers, and still able to delay gratification in pursuit of their goals," says Goleman.[2]

According to Goleman, conventional intelligence or IQ (intelligence quotient) is too narrow and ignores behavior and character. No doubt you have met a person who is extremely bright but socially and emotionally inept. In other words, a high IQ does not guarantee school success.

## Emotional Intelligence

### 8 Ways to Help Your Child Develop His Emotional IQ

1. Coach your child to recognize and identify her feelings. Ask "What made you feel that way?"
2. Teach him to manage his emotions. Children have the power to handle their mood swings. Instruct your child to use "self-talk." Instead of, "I hate Alex because he stole my sandwich," a better way to express his emotions would be, "Alex had a bad day, and that's why he stole my sandwich at lunchtime."
3. Teach your child to control her destructive impulses. Role-play ways to evaluate her choices before acting.
4. Stress the fact that the kind of choices he makes will determine the kind of future he will have.
5. Develop his listening and communication skills. Be certain that your child is aware of ways to communicate nonverbally: tone of voice, gestures, facial expressions, and eye contact.
6. Train her to be a good listener and to express her ideas and emotions clearly.
7. Help him to be assertive rather than aggressive or passive.

8. Teach your child to be kindhearted, self-disciplined, enthusiastic, tolerant, and compassionate.[3]

## 10 Children's Books That Develop Emotional Intelligence

Stories can help children distinguish between their emotions of anger, joy, frustration, and contentment and can help them understand why they feel that way. The following stories reinforce important values such as kindness and compassion. These books provide a safe and secure place for children to sort out their feelings.

1. *Blueberries for Sal* by Robert McCloskey (Viking, 1948) is a Caldecott Honor Book that is appropriate for children in the 3 to 5 year age range. What happens when Little Sal and Little Bear mistakenly trade mothers? Robert McCloskey's gentle, engaging story keeps preschoolers absorbed as Mrs. Bear meets Little Sal and Little Bear surprises Sal's mom. Children will want this book read over and over again, and it is one that an older brother or sister can read if mom or dad needs a break.
2. *Bedtime for Frances* by Russell Hoban (HarperCollins, 1995) is a read-aloud book written for children in preschool. Frances doesn't want to go to bed. It's 7:00 p.m. and the little badger, Frances, is wide awake. And she is using every tactic she can think of to delay turning off the light and going to sleep. Your preschool child will identify with Frances's strategies such as asking "May I have my door open?" and "May I sleep with my teddy bear?"
3. *A Wrinkle in Time* by Madeleine L'Engle (Scholastic) was first published in 1962 and won a Newbery Medal in 1963. The book is written for children ages 9 to 12. The story combines theology, fantasy, and science as characters travel through space and battle against cosmic evil. Meg Murray, her brother Charles Wallace, and a neighbor start on a cosmic journey to find their lost father. The children travel

to the planet Camazotz, where they encounter a repressed society controlled by a disembodied brain that represents evil. Themes include the dangers of unthinking conformity, scientific irresponsibility, and the power of love.

4. *Sideways Stories from Wayside School* by Louis Sachar (Harper Trophy, 2004). The quirky humor of this book makes it a good read-aloud for kids 5 to 12 years old. Your child will love the humor of a thirty-story school that was built sideways, with each classroom stacked on another, and the strange stories with endearing characters. For example, there is the story of Jason, who is stuck to his seat by a large wad of chewing gum, and the teacher who tries to get him unstuck by turning him upside down.

5. *Big Bob and the Thanksgiving Potatoes* by Daniel Pinkwater (Cartwheel, 1999). This book is written for children in the 4 to 8 age range. Life in the second grade is rotten for Big Bob until he makes friends with Big Gloria. When Mr. Salami, the second grade teacher, asks the class to make turkey decorations for Thanksgiving, Big Bob and Big Gloria cook up a scheme to fool him into thinking they are vegetarians. What does a teacher do when his students say they don't believe in eating turkeys? He says, "Make Thanksgiving potatoes." This story helps children think about how it feels to be different, and it tackles a significant subject with humor and imagination. And don't overlook the book's excellent suggestions for helping your child before, during, and after reading the story.

6. *Mrs. Frisby and the Rats of NIMH* by Robert C. O'Brien (Aladdin Paperbacks, 1986). This book is written for children ages 6 and up. The rats of NIMH develop some amazing intellectual powers as subjects in an experimental program. Able to figure out how to unlock their cages, they escape from the laboratory. No longer satisfied with stealing food or living in a sewer, they decide to develop a rat community based on honesty and hard work. With the help of Mrs. Frisby, a field mouse, they avoid recapture and live their dream. This story is written in clear, descriptive

language. The main characters' values include cooperation and loyalty.

7. *Our Only May Amelia* by Jennifer L. Holm (HarperCollins, 1999). This book is appropriate for children in the 9 to 12 age range. Twelve-year-old May Amelia Jacks hates to be told, "Behave like a proper young lady." And why shouldn't she hate it? She works on the family farm as hard as any of her seven teenage brothers, and she thinks and behaves like a boy too. May Amelia's secret birthday wish is for a baby sister. When baby Amy dies, May Amelia goes "grief-mad" and runs away. She returns when she finds out that her family loves her and that her mother and father don't blame her for Amy's death. The book is an accurate account of a Finnish-American family's life in the nineteenth century.

8. *The Amazing Frecktacle* by Ross Venokur (Delacourte Press, 1998). The book is written for children ages 9 and up. Nicholas Bell is mercilessly teased about his freckles by his sixth grade classmates and teacher. He says his freckles must go "because they're ugly! And if I didn't have them, maybe everyone would stop teasing me." Mr. Piddlesticks, a very obnoxious person, offers Nicholas revenge in exchange for his magic freckles. After Nicholas accepts, he finds out that revenge isn't all it's cracked up to be. Children in this age range will understand that the story is a humorous fantasy, and they will appreciate the subtle—and sometimes not-so-subtle—kids' humor.

9. *In the Beginning... The Nearly Complete History of Everything* by Richard Platt (Dorling Kindersley, 1999). The book is written for children ages 9 and up. *In the Beginning...* is a book of inventions, buildings, and achievements. It's a history book children will choose to browse or study, and families will cherish it as a valuable resource. It is a carefully researched volume with more than 2,500 color drawings. The highly visual, attractive format will give children hours of reading pleasure. The biographical index is a bonus, and the subject index makes information easy to find.

10. *The Civil War* by Martin W. Sandler (HarperCollins, 1996). The book is written for children ages 9 to 13. Over one hundred historic black-and-white photographs and illustrations from the Library of Congress bring to life the tragic events of the Civil War. The book is a fascinating record of the camp life, battles, and heroic deeds of men in the Union and Confederate armies. *The Civil War* is a book children will browse or use as a resource for reports. It may be read aloud to children who lack the reading skill or maturity to read it on their own. However, even with older children, it may bring up hard questions that require an adult's answers. The index includes references to photographs and illustrations.

## Learning and Learning Styles

Is your child a visual, auditory, or physical learner? Does he think logically and enjoy math? How are her interpersonal relationships? You probably have noticed that your child prefers a particular learning style. For instance, some children don't listen to directions (auditory) but pay attention when you show them what to do (visual). Other kids must touch, feel, and try it out (physical) before they will completely understand and finish the task.

What difference does it make? To succeed in school, children must use the learning style (seeing, hearing, or physical) that matches their strengths. The first step in understanding a child's educational needs is to determine his or her learning style and areas of strength. Then, if necessary, adjust the educational program to match those strengths.[4]

### Learning Style Inventory

The following thirty-two yes or no statements will help you find out your child's learning style. Use the results as a guide to the ways your child learns.

Learning and Creativity

| Visual Indicators | (Circle One) | |
|---|---|---|
| Likes to operate a computer | Yes | No |
| Daydreams | Yes | No |
| Enjoys drawing | Yes | No |
| Reads books for fun | Yes | No |
| Reads instructions | Yes | No |
| Says, "Show me." | Yes | No |
| Spelling is easy | Yes | No |
| Looks at pictures | Yes | No |
| Likes to tell stories and jokes | Yes | No |
| Remembers trivia | Yes | No |
| **Auditory Indicators** | **(Circle One)** | |
| Listens to directions | Yes | No |
| Says, "Tell me." | Yes | No |
| Says, "I hear you." | Yes | No |
| You say, "Listen to me." | Yes | No |
| Listens to her friends | Yes | No |
| Follows her friend's directions | Yes | No |
| Always on the phone | Yes | No |
| Constantly listens to music | Yes | No |
| Shouts when angry | Yes | No |
| **Physical Indicators** | **(Circle One)** | |
| Remembers names | Yes | No |
| Memorizes by repeating key words | Yes | No |
| Main interest is talking to friends | Yes | No |
| Learns by trial and error | Yes | No |
| Says, "Let me try it." | Yes | No |
| Shows rather than tells | Yes | No |
| Likes tools and gadgets | Yes | No |
| Follows his instinct | Yes | No |
| Likes physical activities and sports | Yes | No |
| Moves in time to music | Yes | No |
| Moves around when studying | Yes | No |
| Moves around when anxious | Yes | No |
| Stomps and slams doors when angry | Yes | No |

45

**Scoring:** Count how many of the visual, auditory, and physical "yes" statements you circled and place the sum for each category in the section below.

Totals: Visual_____     Auditory_____     Physical_____

My child's learning strengths are:

_____

_____

_____

Is my child using the learning style she prefers?

_____

_____

What can I do to improve the way my child learns?

_____

_____

_____

The total scores indicate your child's learning style preference and will give you a hint about the way your child learns. The above questions have no right or wrong answers. Use the totals and your answers to the three questions to evaluate how your child learns. Then if you have concerns about your child's learning and school success, make an appointment with his teacher.

## Teach Your Child Persistence

Persistence is an important trait for school success. Like all of us, kids get discouraged and want to give up or quit when they don't find an easy solution to a problem. As your child's role model, you can show him how to be persistent by modeling persistence.

Here are some tips to help children in various age groups learn to be more persistent in their school projects and homework.

### *Preschool*

- Know the limits of your child's attention span. Young children can stay with a task only a few minutes before their attention wanders off.
- Your child's behavior will tell you when she is ready to go on to something else.
- If your son asks to help you, give him a task and make sure he completes it.
- If your daughter hasn't finished a job, call her back and talk about it. If it is important, insist that she finish.

### *Primary Grades*

- Limit your child's work periods so he can achieve success before he tires.
- Reduce distractions when your child is reading, solving puzzles, or writing a story. Set a special time each day for your child's school projects.
- Provide time for creative activities like music appreciation, drawing, and dramatic play.
- Reward your child for her accomplishments. Use a magnet to place her poem on the refrigerator. Read her story to the family.

### *Upper Grades*

- Let him work on his own. Don't help him unless he asks for it.
- Be certain that your child knows how to use the computer for research.

- Be a good model. Explain how long it takes you to accomplish a task and show the completed product.
- Don't preach a sermon about persistence. Teach by your example.

## Creativity: Learning's Spark Plug

### The Truth about Creativity: A Quiz

How well do you understand creative thinking? Let's consider a few myths about creativity and creative thinking. Many of the myths are hard-core ones, and if you accept them, they will affect the way you approach your own child's creativity. The following quiz will help you separate fact from fiction.

Read each statement and jot down the letter of the answer you think is correct.

1. When the teacher says Jimmy's ideas are creative, she means
   (a) he knows ten ways to get out of homework
   (b) he's a tricky little guy
   (c) he's a math genius
   (d) he thinks differently than other children
2. Sarah finishes her assignment in fifteen minutes, then wanders around the classroom. This is a sign
   (a) that she is bored
   (b) that she took a speed-reading class
   (c) that her IQ is out of this world
   (d) of nothing to do with creative thinking
3. The twins are scatterbrained and fail to follow through on their ideas. Their teacher is correct when he says
   (a) the twins are highly creative
   (b) this is typical behavior for twins
   (c) they eat too much junk food
   (d) only ideas that result in a product are creative

4. Jake plods along in class. He does what he is asked to do and nothing more. He won't try new games or activities. His parents are correct in believing that

(a) Jake's creative talents will surface

(b) he is creative but shy

(c) he is a prodigy waiting to be discovered

(d) unless he is encouraged he will lose his creative gift

5. Emma's parents know she is creative, and they are waiting for her to blossom. Her parents are

(a) right—creative ideas come out of the blue

(b) right—that's the way Albert Einstein developed

(c) right—creative people study

(d) wrong—sometimes years of preparation precede a creative product

6. No one in Bobby's class understands what he is talking about, including his teacher. His mom and dad believe he is creative because

(a) his complex thinking proves that he is creative

(b) his doctor says, "Cut out the sugar"

(c) only complex ideas are creative

(d) often simple ideas are creative ones

7. June's dad doesn't believe she is creative. He says everything that is useful has already been invented. This is

(a) true—new ideas are reworked old ones

(b) true—normal people aren't inventors

(c) true—children can't think creatively

(d) false—some simple ideas are big winners

If you answered letter (d) for all the questions, you were 100 percent correct, and you can tell the difference between legend and truth.[5] Now read on for more about myths about creative thinking.

## Myths about Creative Thinking

In his book *Imagineering*, Michael LeBoeuf lists several myths about creativity.[6]

### Myth 1: To Be Creative Means Imagining or Doing Something New

If you believe this myth, you may miss out on the fun of watching your child's creativity grow. Most experts define creative thinking as the way your child approaches and solves problems.

### Myth 2: Only a Genius Is Creative

Some individuals with high IQs are extremely creative at what they do, while the opposite is also true. The high-IQ person can be a rigid, noncreative thinker since intelligence test results reveal little about creative thinking.

### Myth 3: Creativity Is Impractical and Borders on Insanity

The test of a creative idea is its usefulness. The source of creativity is good mental health. Children need the freedom to risk new ideas. Low self-esteem, anxiety, and fear are creativity killers.

### Myth 4: If You Have Creative Ability, Your Talents Will Be Discovered

Children's creativity thrives on motivation, encouragement, and praise. Without encouragement, their creative talents may be hidden under a blanket of anxiety and low self-esteem.

### Myth 5: Creativity Means Complexity

If this statement were true, some of the essential products we use might not exist. For example, something as simple yet useful as masking tape wasn't invented until 1925.

## Myth 6: The Best Way Has Already Been Found

The adhesive bandage, safety pin, paper cup, and soda can pop-top are examples of imagination, curiosity, common sense, and hard work. Or think about more recent inventions like the thumb drive—a small, portable storage device that plugs in to your computer's USB port.

### 5 Facts about Your Child's Creative Abilities

Parents often are confused by terms like "gifted," "talented," and "creative." Children sometimes fool us. The child we think is creative because of high IQ, high grades, and good behavior may be less creative than the child whose grades are average. Here's why.

1. Intelligence tests are poor measures of creativity.
2. Distinctive traits of creative children are intuition, flexibility, social poise, and lack of concern for social norms. The relationship between good grades and creativity is low.
3. Gifted and talented children may need training to improve their creative thinking.
4. There is an overlap between the skills of gifted, talented, and creative children.
5. Talented children have special gifts that require nurturing and cultivating.

### 8 Ways Parents Can Encourage Their Child's Creativity

1. Set an example. Forget about perfection. Listen to your child's interests, and share your own ideas with your child.
2. Encourage your child's creative abilities by eliminating parenting practices that offer too much freedom or set impossible limits.
3. Be enthusiastic and encourage good work habits.
4. Avoid authoritarian parenting. There is a difference between parents who assert their authority and parents who are authoritarian. Research has shown that children

of authoritarian parents are less creative than other children.

5. Set limits. Creative behavior is not enhanced by allowing children to do as they please.

6. It's easy to miss the creative expressions of children. Listen to what your child says.

7. Let your child express his ideas; don't belittle them.

8. All creative individuals are curious. Curiosity is one of the most important traits shared by children and adults. If you want your child to become a creative adult, don't ignore this trait.

## Ways to Improve Creative Imagination

### Preschool

1. Make games out of everyday events. If your tot makes noises like a cat or dog, invent a game about animals.

2. Help your child enjoy imaginative play. Plan a mini-drama with your child playing one character and you another. Use hand puppets and other toys that encourage creative thinking.

3. Keep on hand watercolor paints, colored marking pens, plain and colored paper, and other art materials. Allow time to experiment with design and colors. Don't insist that your child draw a house, an animal, and so on.

4. Play music while your child is at play, and sing along with him. Help him think up a new melody or new words to the song you are singing.

### Primary Grades

1. Invent stories built around your child's imaginary playmates. Use cars, trucks, dolls, and other playthings to enhance the stories.

2. Read imagination-stretching stories to your child.

3. Make up plays and act them out with other family members.

4. Together dream up an invention. Name the invention and draw a picture of it.
5. Children enjoy playing with codes. Help your child invent a secret code. Check with your librarian for a book of codes.
6. Try some flip-flops. Ask your child to imagine what would happen if fish flew and birds swam? Or dogs hopped and rabbits barked?

### Upper Grades

1. Begin more detailed story writing. Avoid simply relating events; try developing a story plot and characters.
2. Ask your child to invent a new game.
3. Ask your child to design a "fun machine." What makes it fun?
4. Design a code using pictures and letters. Clip secret messages to the fridge or family bulletin board.[7]

## Go "Imagineering": A Game for Early Elementary Children

Look through newspapers and magazines for pictures of different kinds of balloons. Cut them out and glue them to a piece of paper. Stretch out on the floor with your child, get comfortable, and imagine you are balloons: Slowly fill with air. How does it feel to puff up and sail away? Go up and bump the ceiling . . . slowly float down . . . watch out for the nail on the wall . . . ouch! Did it hurt when the nail stuck you? I'm leaking air. Are you? Let's float gently to the floor. Let all your air out and relax. Would you like to be a balloon again?

Write your own Imagineering game. Don't make the game too long; the limit for many children is about ten minutes.[8]

## A Good Laugh Helps to Clear the Air

A home that honors humor is a lively place to live. Tom Mullen, author of *Laughing Out Loud*, says, "Parents usually recognize a happy child when they see, hear, and clean up after one. Spilled milk is regarded by few children as a calamity. . . . Children teach us that pleasant things are to be enjoyed and disagreeable things, so long as they don't spoil the fun, acquire a pleasant flavor and provoke a laugh."[9] Why not let humor, off-the-wall ideas, and respect for creative thinking be a way of life for your family?

### 14 Ways to Increase the Use of Humor in Your Home

Preschool

1. Laugh together when something funny happens.
2. Make a joke when your child puts her arm in the wrong sleeve or a shoe on the wrong foot, then gently correct the mistake.
3. Have a good laugh when your child plays a joke on you.
4. Together read children's riddle and joke books. Let him change the endings of jokes and riddles.

Primary Grades

5. Share family jokes.
6. Act out humorous situations and videotape them.
7. Start your home joke library.
8. Loosen up and have fun with your children's jokes and funny behavior.

Upper Grades

9. Ask your child to draw the funniest thing that ever happened.
10. Have a joke-of-the-week bulletin board and post the best jokes on it.
11. Plan a family comedy night. Let the child who writes a funny story or joke read it to the rest of the family.

## Backward Humor

Beginning with infants and toddlers, kids find doing something the wrong way hilarious.

For instance, the game "Drop it" that infants seem to learn without coaching. "Drop it" starts when your infant grabs a feeding spoon full of strained spinach, looks you in the eye, and tosses it over the side of the highchair. As far-fetched as it seems, some parents aren't aware of the game until the spoon hits the floor three or four times.[10]

12. Honor laughter and refuse to let TV be your guide to family fun.
13. Keep humor healthy and fun. Children are bombarded with all kinds of humor. Hostile insults or destructive jokes shouldn't be tolerated.[11]

# 4

# Home and School Safety

## Ways to Improve Internet Safety

Blocking and filtering software helps parents find and delete unwanted websites in favor of programs that are fun and educational. However, this software may give parents a false sense of security, since computer whiz kids can figure out how to turn controls off and on, say experts. Still, the best way to block or to filter what your child sees on the Internet is to station the computer in the living room or family room where you can keep an eye on what is being watched.

But the good news is that watchful parents can assure that their children use the incredible information resources of the Internet without encountering dirty words, instructions on how to make a bomb, or a pervert's website.

### 6 Internet Safety Rules for Kids

1. Never reply to offensive, strange, mean, or upsetting email messages.

2. Never give my home address, telephone number, parent's work address, or credit card number without my mom or dad's permission.
3. Always ask for my parent's permission before I agree to meet anyone anywhere.
4. Never give my family's Internet account password to anyone.
5. Never send scanned pictures of my family or me to anyone without my parent's approval.
6. Stop right away if I see or read something on a website that upsets or offends me.[1]

## Blocking and Filtering Software

1. Cybersitter 9.0 is a five-time winner of *PC Magazine*'s Editors' Choice award. Cybersitter is designed primarily for home use, and it is easy to install even for the novice computer user. Nevertheless, it has many advanced filtering features.
2. Cyber Patrol 7 filters and monitors software and helps parents control their child's computer usage. The filtering can be defeated at times by a determined user, but in such instances the handy Web log will show you where the offender went online. Multilayered filtering techniques are very effective. Numerous options are available for customizing filtering on a user-by-user or system-wide basis. Time limits and usage monitoring are included.
3. Net Nanny Parental Controls received the 2007 "Top Ten Reviews Gold Award" for Internet filter software. Net Nanny includes email filtering and the ability to create a customized blocked list of applications.
4. WebWatcher is a complete suite of features, but the program's strong point is its ability to monitor and block websites. WebWatcher is a Web-based program that allows parents to view all of the Internet activity that takes place on the computer being monitored.

## Promote After-School Safety

The warning *come straight home from school* hardly seems strong enough in light of the almost daily headlines screaming of children lured away by strangers. However, thousands of children in risky situations are not abducted because they know what to do in dangerous situations.

The National Center for Missing and Exploited Children recommends that "every home and school should teach children about safety and protection measures. As a parent, you should take an active interest in your children and listen to them. Teach your children that they can be assertive in order to protect themselves against abduction and exploitation. And most importantly, make your home a place of trust and support that fulfills your child's needs."[2]

### 7 Steps to After-School Safety

To help your school-age child avoid risky situations, follow these safety tips from the National Center for Missing and Exploited Children and other sources.

1. Always know where your children are.
2. Have your children check with you before they go anywhere or do anything. Ask for regular check-ins with you or a trusted adult when you're not with them.
3. Remember that nothing takes the place of your supervision of your own children.
4. Teach your child that if a stranger grabs her, she should scream, "This man is trying to take me away," or "This is not my daddy."
5. Role-play dangerous situations. Ask you child what he should do if:
   (a) a driver stops his car and says, "Your mom's hurt. Come on and get in, and I'll take you to the hospital."
   (b) a woman says, "Please help me find my puppy."

(c) a person promises, "I'll give you five dollars to carry a package to my car."
6. Protect against bogus friends or relatives: choose a family password. Teach your child not to get into a car with someone who doesn't know the password.
7. Organize neighborhood "safe houses." Enlist neighbors willing to shelter frightened or threatened children. Instruct your child to run to a safe house if he is scared.

## Safety Rules for Parents and Children

The National Center for Missing and Exploited Children advises: "Be careful when you put your child's name on clothing, backpacks, lunch boxes or bicycle license plates. If a child's name is visible it may put them on a 'first name' basis with abductor.

"Walk the route to and from school with your children, pointing out landmarks and safe places to go if they're being followed or need help. Make a map with your children showing acceptable routes to school, using main roads and avoiding shortcuts or isolated areas. If your children take a bus, visit the bus stop with them and make sure they know which bus to take."[3]

## 6 Ways to Protect Your Preschool Child's Safety

1. Be certain your child knows his name, address, and telephone number and the names of his parents.
2. Make it a rule that he always takes a friend with him when he goes outside to play.
3. Teach your child to yell "Stop it!" if someone tries to touch her or treat her in a way that scares her, confuses her, or makes her feel uncomfortable.
4. Be sure your child knows he can tell you or a trusted adult if he feels scared, uncomfortable, or confused.
5. Enforce the rule, "Don't go out alone." Remember, there is safety in numbers.

6. Teach your child that she must always tell an adult where she is going.

## Bullies and Out-of-Sync Children

Out-of-sync children have no special friends to save them a place on the school bus or to sit by in the lunchroom. Children mimic them and label them with cruel nicknames. Writer Tim Larimer describes the pain kids suffer when they are bullied. For a week he traveled with a group of kids on their class trip to Washington, DC. During that week he rode busses, ate Big Macs, and talked and listened to a group of seventh and eighth graders. He chronicled the discomfort and pain of Ellen and Ricky, two students who didn't fit in. When Ellen cracked jokes, no one laughed. Ricky was told to "Go away and leave us alone" when he walked up to a group of classmates.

As a school psychologist I have observed and counseled out-of-sync children. They are often mimicked behind their backs and labeled with cruel nicknames like "retard" and "loser."[4]

Psychologist Jennifer Shroff Pendley said, "Being bullied can also have long-term consequences, affecting the way children form relationships as adolescents and adults and even possibly leading to more serious problems like substance abuse and depression. In addition, bully victims are more likely to experience withdrawn behavior such as anxiety and depression."[5]

### Ways Kids Bully Other Children

1. *Emotional bullying* is more common among girls and includes shunning and spreading rumors about their victim.
2. *Verbal bullying* includes name-calling, mocking, and laughing at the child's expense.

3. *Physical bullying* often follows a verbally abusive bully's attack on a child he considers physically weak. The physical bully may kick, hit, pinch, pull hair, or threaten physical harm to the other child.
4. *Cyberbullying* is a new phenomenon that surfaced as communication technologies advanced. Kids bully others by spreading hurtful information through email, Internet chat rooms, and electronic gadgets. Bullies can hassle their victims at all hours.
5. *Racist bullies* tell racial jokes and make fun of another child's cultural traditions, skin color, or word pronunciation.
6. *Sexual bullying* involves all kinds of unwanted physical contact or sexually abusive or unsuitable comments.

## 7 Signs of a Bullied Child

1. Unexplained bumps and bruises. (*"I don't know what happened."*)
2. Mysterious illnesses or multiple reasons for not going to school. (*"My stomach aches"; "I have a headache"; "I think I'm going to throw up."*)
3. Changes in her eating or sleeping patterns. (*"I can't go to sleep, I'm afraid I'll have bad dreams"; "I'm just not hungry."*)
4. Body language—he hangs his head, hunches his shoulders, and avoids eye contact.
5. Missing money, damaged homework, or missing articles from his backpack. (*"I don't know where it went; I guess I just lost it."*)
6. Signs of school phobia: she doesn't want to go to school, comes home early, and skips classes. (*"I don't like school"; "I wish I could quit."*)
7. Crying at a moment's notice and mood swings varying from happy to sad. Feelings of hopelessness. (*"I'll never get out of special education."*)

## 8 Questions to Ask a Child You Suspect Is Being Bullied

1. What's it like to walk home from school?
2. What's it like waiting at the bus stop?
3. What's it like riding the bus to or from school?
4. What happens on the playground at recess or before school starts?
5. Have school bullies threatened anyone you know?
6. What happens in the hall between classes or at lunch-time?
7. Have neighborhood or school bullies bothered anyone you know?
8. Do you know any kid who receives threatening, insulting, or dirty emails, instant messages, or text messages?

## 6 Ways to Comfort a Bullied Child

1. Offer comfort by listening to your child.
2. Talk about the problem and how you can help.
3. Don't add to the problem by showing your anger.
4. Ask how she feels about being bullied. If she is angry, let her express her anger.
5. Explain to your child that he isn't to blame.
6. Be sure to confirm your child's feelings; they are genuine.

## 8 Myths and Misconceptions about School Bullies

1. *Ignore bullying and it will go away.* Experience shows that bullying doesn't stop if the victim tries to ignore it. Instead, ignoring it encourages the bully to intensify his or her tactics, and the torment gets worse. Encourage your child to keep a log of events, and schedule a parent-teacher conference.
2. *Bullying toughens up the victim.* Bullying causes trauma, and if not handled properly, it can affect the child for life. It may lower your child's educational achievement, cause health problems, and produce psychological injury.

3. *The child should accept it as a part of life.* All kinds of abuse, including harassment, violence, and physical abuse, are unacceptable parts of life.
4. *Victims should retaliate.* The bully may stop for a while if she is confronted by a teacher or other adult. But children know that if they retaliate, the bullying will only get worse.
5. *Bullies are psychologically strong.* Not true. Bullies are weak and emotionally immature, and they compensate for their weakness with aggression.
6. *Victims are unlikable.* Between 50 and 75 percent of children are bullied in school, and the bullies are always disliked.
7. *Bullied children grow up to be tougher adults.* This is a rationalization. Bullies use it to justify and excuse their actions. Bullying causes physical, psychological, and emotional injuries.
8. *Victims of bullies are wimps.* The victims of bullies tend to be sensitive, intelligent, respectful, creative children with a strong sense of fair play and integrity. They don't like violence.

## 10 Reasons Children Fear School

The April 2000 issue of *USA Weekend* reported the results of a survey of nearly 130,000 students in grades six to twelve who were quizzed on school life. Here are some of the highlights of this eye-opening survey's findings.

- *1 in 5* has felt fear since the fatal shootings at Columbine High School in 1999. The younger boys and girls were the most fearful.
- *1 in 4* say they were intentionally struck by another student. Nearly 4 in 10 boys said they were struck.
- *4 in 10* have guns in their homes, and more than half could access the guns.
- *7 in 10* would feel happier if schools were safer and say they would learn more too.
- *3 in 4* report that fights are provoked by small incidents such as a glance or bump into another person.

64

- *3 in 10* have been physically threatened.
- *8 in 10* have seen a school fight.
- *1 in 10* say students carry weapons to school.
- *77 percent* surveyed say they would be happier if they felt safer at school.
- *91 percent* say they've seen students picked on in the past year.
- Solutions: *4 in 10* want the bad kids sent away, and *1 in 5* think metal detectors would help.[6]

## Cyberbullying

Cyberbullying has surfaced as communication technologies have advanced. Kids bully others by spreading hurtful information through email, Internet chat rooms, and electronic gadgets. As one article put it, "Cyber bullying did not exist a few years ago. Camera cell phones, instant messaging, online social networking sites, and a host of other technologies now can be exploited with relative ease to create 24/7 harassment. . . . Cyber bullying is a growing problem in the United States—one in three teens and one of six preteens are victims of cyber bullying according to a recent national poll conducted by law enforcement officers. Alarmingly, students are twice as likely to be bullied online as opposed to face-to-face."[7]

### Types of Cyberbullying

1. *Cyberstalking.* Sending harassing messages that may include threats of bodily harm.
2. *Denigration.* Sending or posting hateful messages about a person or a group of people.
3. *Flaming.* Sending hateful messages or images including pictures taken with a cell phone to a private person or group.
4. *Harassment.* Repeatedly sending offensive messages.

5. *Impersonation.* Sending messages under someone else's identity that make him or her look bad or place the person in danger.
6. *Outing.* Sending or posting material about a person that contains sensitive or private information.
7. Trickery. Fooling someone into revealing personal information and then distributing the material.

### 5 Ways Parents Can Help

1. Attach rules to the use of your child's computer or cell phone.
2. Move your child's computer out of the bedroom into the family room or living room.
3. Teach your child not to share passwords.
4. Install monitoring and filtering software. Check out the free downloads at k9webprotection.com and safefamilies.org.
5. If your child is cyberbullied, save and print out the evidence. Decide together where to go for help.[8]

### An Example of Cyberbullying

DIVAGIRL:       "Hey loser, watch your back."
SURFERCHICK:  "What r u talking about?"
DIVAGIRL:       "Why don't you kill yourself while u r ahead?"
SURFERCHICK:  "Why can't you just leave me alone?"
DIVAGIRL:       "Ugly girls like you need to be put in their place."[9]

### How Common Is Cyberbullying?

- 90 percent of middle school students have had their feelings hurt online.
- 75 percent have visited a website bashing another student.

66

- 40 percent have had their passwords stolen and changed by a bully who then locked them out of their own account or sent communications posing as them.
- Only 15 percent of parents polled knew what cyberbullying was.[10]

## Bullying Checklist

Use the following checklist to help determine if your child is a bully or is being bullied by another child.

| Signs that your child is a bully | True | False |
| --- | --- | --- |
| Lacks self-confidence | ___ | ___ |
| Spreads rumors | ___ | ___ |
| Mocks other children | ___ | ___ |
| Fights and threatens harm | ___ | ___ |
| Shuns unpopular children | ___ | ___ |
| Makes racial slurs | ___ | ___ |
| Laughs at the expense of others | ___ | ___ |

| Signs that your child is being bullied | True | False |
| --- | --- | --- |
| Invents illnesses to escape from school | ___ | ___ |
| Loses belongings or money | ___ | ___ |
| Stays awake after bedtime | ___ | ___ |
| Wets the bed | ___ | ___ |
| Finds it difficult to concentrate | ___ | ___ |
| Irritable | ___ | ___ |
| Problems with schoolwork | ___ | ___ |
| Begs for a ride to school | ___ | ___ |

*Reasons I think my child is being bullied:*

1. _____

_____

2. _____

_____

3. _____

_____

*How I plan to help my child overcome being bullied:*

1. _____

_____

2. _____

_____

3. _____

_____

*Reasons I think my child may be a bully:*

1. _____

_____

2. _____

_____

3. _____

_____

*How I plan to stop my child's bullying:*

1. _____

   _____

2. _____

   _____

3. _____

   _____

# 5

# Effective Discipline

It's easy to find a remedy for the whining child who is hungry or cold or needs a nap: feed her, wrap her in a cozy blanket, or put her to bed. You have met her needs, and the complaining stops. But what about the whiny-voiced kid who moans and groans until she gets what she wants? Or what can you do about the picky eater who tries your patience?

When the grandparents of my children visited, the eating habits of my daughter often dominated the table talk. She was a picky eater. And it didn't matter whether her tummy was full or she simply wasn't hungry—her grandma would comment on her untouched food. Once, after failing to coax her to eat, her grandmother picked up my daughter's fork, stabbed a veggie, and began to feed her. Of course our daughter delighted in the attention, while I squirmed in my chair and did a slow burn. I wanted to scream, "Don't do that. She's ten years old!" But of course I couldn't say a word without causing a major scene.

Looking back, a picky eaters policy for our family would have helped. With a policy in place, we could have discussed our daughter's eating likes and dislikes and her reward for finishing her meal.

Rewards are a better way to control your kids than giving them goodies to quiet them down or to stop the arguing. "Rewards actually can have a legitimate place in parenting. How and when you give 'payment' is what matters. Bottom line: You want to use rewards to help your kids to learn habits that will stick, not disappear as soon as the rewards are gone," said Virginia M. Shiller, author of *Rewards for Kids! Ready-to-Use Charts and Activities for Positive Parenting*.[1]

## Guidelines for Effective Discipline

1. *Be honest about how you feel.* Tell your child exactly how you feel about his behavior, but don't berate or accuse him.
2. *Choose rewards that work.* Find out what your child likes, and if you don't know, ask him. Often the reason nothing seems to work is because the reward is wrong or it is applied inconsistently.
3. *Recognize success.* Saving up your rewards for a day or more will only slow your child's progress. Be consistent with your rewards and eliminate responses such as "Not now, I'm busy," or "Wait until tomorrow."
4. *Praise an accomplishment.* When your child isn't whining, reward her. Don't expect a positive change in your child's behavior if you stick to the agreement one day and forget about it for the next few days.
5. *Claim the right to pass.* Rather than letting your anger boil over or relenting and allowing your child to continue her misbehavior, wait for a better time to discuss the problem.
6. *Remember.* By putting an end to unacceptable behavior, the whole atmosphere of your family life will change. When problems are solved with calm obedience and respectful

negotiation, everyone benefits, say Dr. Scott Turansky and Joanne Miller, authors of the tape series *Parenting Is Heart Work.*[2]

## Rewards for Appropriate Behavior

As a school psychologist with thirty years of experience in education, I've worked with children who have whined, complained, pouted, and sometimes refused to obey parents and teachers. I participated in weekly Child Study Team meetings to discuss the children who weren't succeeding in school.

These children weren't interested in anything their teachers or parents suggested. Often parents told me, "I've tried everything, and nothing works." I believe that nothing worked because the rewards, or reinforcers, selected by parents and teachers weren't important to these kids. When the kids were offered a reinforcer that meant something to them, their behavior usually changed.

### Examples of Rewards

1. A compliment
2. A hug
3. Helping someone complete a chore
4. Finishing homework on time
5. Free time
6. Money
7. A trip to a fast-food restaurant
8. Winning a prize
9. Staying up past bedtime

There are two types of rewards. Some children respond to an immediate reward they can taste, touch, or buy, such as money, a trip to McDonald's, a prize, or a chance to stay up past their bedtime. Other children are rewarded when they reach an important personal goal.

Stanford University psychologist John D. Krumboltz states that to solve many children's behavior problems, "Arrange for an immediate reward after each correct performance. And under most circumstances the sooner the reinforcer is presented after the correct behavior, the sooner the child learns the desired behavior."[3]

### How to Use Rewards

| Child's Behvior | Reward | Parent's Response |
| --- | --- | --- |
| 1. Works and learns without being pushed | Give a compliment | Help your child if she asks for it |
| 2. Works only if rewarded | Encourage new interests | Don't offer rewards Support your child's ideas |
| 3. Refuses to go to sleep | More free time | Encourage your child's special interests |
| 4. Her goal is to make money | Emphasize your child's accomplishment | Check your values |
| 5. Does the activity if told he must do it | Examine whether the activity is too hard or boring | Try to build self-confidence |
| 6. Enjoys a challenge | Give her room to think and experiment | Respect your child's ideas |
| 7. Afraid to start something new | Praise initiatives | Encourage assertive behavior |

### 5 Guidelines for a Workable Reward Plan

Unless you find a way to motivate your child to do her homework or other tasks, chances are good she won't do it. The following guidelines will help you set up a reward program that reinforces better behavior.

74

1. Don't talk about a reward system when you or your child is angry or upset. Wait until the timing is better.
2. Don't preach or nag about undone tasks.
3. Don't set up long-term goals; choose short-term goals that lead to the desired behavior.
4. Don't think you have failed if your child slips or misbehaves. Remind him of his successes and encourage him to continue.
5. Reevaluate your plan if your child loses interest and the old behavior continues.

## *Rewards for Preschool and Elementary School Kids*

Before starting a family reward program, be sure to talk it over with your children. It will be easier if your kids are enthusiastic about it, but start the program even if they grumble. Use the following rewards as behavior reinforcers.

### Preschool Children

1. Play a game with her parents
2. Plan a picnic
3. Go someplace special with mom or dad
4. Plan a trip to the fire station
5. Plan a swimming trip
6. Have a special dessert
7. Rent a video
8. Read a bedtime story
9. Be rocked by grandma or grandpa
10. Stay up late
11. Plan the breakfast menu
12. Do a puppet play

### Early Elementary School Children

13. Go to a movie with a friend
14. Feed the baby
15. Eat out
16. Go to a baseball game with grandpa

17. Plan a trip to Disneyland or to a theme park
18. Spend the night with a friend
19. Take time off from chores
20. Decorate his own room
21. Go skating or swimming
22. Feed a pet
23. Play a game
24. Order pizza
25. Extra computer time
26. Listen to his or her iPod

### Late Elementary School Children

27. Go to a concert with a parent and a friend
28. Make a detailed plan for summer vacation
29. Take babysitting lessons
30. Help with young children (4-H club, Scouts, church, or school)
31. Go to the mall
32. Extra TV time
33. Meet friends at the movies
34. Stop at a friend's house after school

## Teach Self-Control

Children can learn to make good choices, unless their parents, teachers, and other adults make too many choices for them. By learning to control their own behavior, children will learn what is right regardless of their peers' behavior.

### Ways to Teach Self-Control

1. *Take a break.* When your child is angry, help her to calm down and stay in control. Try a change of activity or a time-out period. Wait to talk about it until she is calm.

2. *Use specific activities that teach self-control.* Young children can learn to control their behavior by role-playing a problem using hand puppets.
3. *Use appropriate rewards.* Give consistent, positive feedback to teach appropriate behavior. Remember that a parent's praise and attention are highly regarded by children.
4. *Stop interruptions.* If your child is starved for attention, he or she likely will interrupt conversations inappropriately. Teach her to wait until others aren't talking before she joins in.[4]

## Strategies to Teach Better Behavior

### Use a Behavior Contract

Disciplining children isn't fun, but a behavior contract will help you develop the kind of behavior you expect from your child. A *When-Then* behavior contract will give your children a clear idea of the rewards and consequences of their behavior.

### Sample When-Then Contract

#### Charlene's Contract

**Problem:** Charlene whines when she is asked to do her homework.

**Required Behavior:** *When* Charlene completes her homework without whining, *then* she will receive 30 minutes of free TV time.

**Consequences:** If she continues to whine, *then* she will lose TV privileges for one day.

**Date:** _____

**Signed (Child)** _____

**Signed (Parent)** _____

77

When using a behavior contract, remember:

1. Your child must successfully complete a goal to receive a reward.
2. The contract must clearly state the reward for successful completion and the consequences if the contract is not completed successfully.
3. You and your child must sign the contract.
4. If your child resists, it's your job to hold the line.

## Practice Problem Solving

Andrea loved kindergarten, but during the ride home on the school bus she ran up and down the aisles and refused to sit in her seat. The bus driver said that unless Andrea stayed in her seat, she would have to walk home.

What is your solution to Andrea's behavior? List and evaluate your ideas. To help you get started, the problem and the first idea are stated below.

**Problem (stated in one sentence):** Andrea won't stay in her seat on the school bus.

| Ideas (possible solutions) | Plus (positive consequences) | Minus (negative consequences) | Final Solution |
| --- | --- | --- | --- |
| 1. Talk to her teacher | 1. A reward for a good report | 1. Let her walk home | 1. Let Andrea choose the solution |
| 2. | | | |
| 3. | | | |
| 4. | | | |
| 5. | | | |

## Handling School-Related Problems

If your child is having trouble at school, talk to your child's teacher. As a school psychologist, I know how vital parent-teacher conferences are to a child's education. Regular attendance is a must, even if you know it is going to be an unpleasant meeting. By keeping close contact with your child's teacher, you may be assured that your child will progress academically and socially. The teacher needs to know things such as:

1. Any major changes at home
2. The medication your child takes, when she takes each dose, and the directions for administering it
3. Ways the teacher can help her
4. The concerns you have about his behavior

### 6 Do's and Don'ts for Parents Meeting with Teachers

1. Do bring a list to ensure discussion of your major concerns.
2. Do bring a pencil and notebook and jot down comments, information, suggestions, action items, and follow-up items you want to remember.
3. Do ask for specific ways that you can help your child at home. Then check back regularly for the teacher's comments.
4. Don't be late or miss your appointment. Your appointment probably isn't the only one the teacher has scheduled; being late might keep you from discussing critical issues vital to your child's education. And don't bring up a burning question two minutes before the conference ends.
5. Do talk to your child about the conference. Before the conference ask her if she has questions for the teacher. Afterward, explain the decisions made and how you believe they will help her at school.
6. Don't be confrontational with the teacher if you are dissatisfied with your child's progress. Have a cooperative attitude

79

and try to work out problems together. But if you aren't able to solve a problem, ask to have an administrator sit in at a follow-up conference.

## When Siblings Argue

A parent's request can easily turn into an argument that ends with both the parent and the child angry and unhappy. And the odds are that it will turn into combat involving the parent and the siblings. Does the following scene sound familiar?

MOM: "Ginger, come and set the table. It's your turn."

DAUGHTER: "Mom, it's not my turn; it's Scott's."

MOM: "I need it set now. I'll talk to Scott later."

DAUGHTER: "But Mom, that's not fair. It's his turn to set the table, and I'm not going to do it."

MOM: "Yes, you are!"

DAUGHTER: "I won't. It's not my turn."

Remember, it takes two to start an argument. If a similar situation comes up in your family, try the following ways to control an argument:

1. Design a weekly chart labeled "Tasks to Be Completed" that shows the child responsible for each task. Choose a reward for the child who completes a week's work without arguing.
2. Try having your children do the same chore together. This method may eliminate arguing and enhance cooperation between the siblings.
3. Teach your child that it takes two to argue. If he doesn't answer back, the other person is just talking to herself.

80

4. Say it once. State your case and then be quiet. If you ask your son to do a chore, ask just once, and then ignore his argument. Let him get used to "That's final."
5. Accept a little complaining if it is done respectfully. Listen, but don't answer back.
6. Offer choices but not commands. For instance, "Would you like to do your homework or unload the dishwasher?" Remember that to answer "Neither" isn't a valid choice.

# 6

# Recognizing Problems

Children face numerous problems daily, and often the way they handle these problems depends on how they feel about themselves. This chapter will help you recognize some of the problems children face and remedies for them.

## Self-Esteem

Parents have an enormous effect on their child's self-esteem. A child's self-esteem and body image indicate how he values himself. It includes self-pride, feelings of worth, and how the child accepts his or her own appearance. You rarely if ever will hear comments like "I'm too skinny" or "I wish my hair was pretty like hers" from a child with a healthy self-image.

You may love, accept, and approve of your child, but unless those feelings filter through to your youngster, he will not believe he measures up to your standards. A healthy self-esteem is a major key to school success, and it is the child's armor against the daily challenges kids face. Children with high self-esteem have a better chance of being successful than those who feel worthless and unloved.

### 7 Reasons a Positive Self-Esteem Leads to Success

1. Children with high self-esteem act independently and responsibly.
2. High self-esteem children take pride in their accomplishments.
3. They feel loved by their family.
4. They control their positive and negative emotions.
5. They're not reluctant to help others.
6. They have pride in their accomplishments.
7. If they fail at a task, they keep trying until they succeed.

### Children with Low Self-Esteem

Children with low self-esteem may appear to be well-adjusted, but their attitude oozes defeat. Here are some signs of low self-esteem:

1. When challenged they become frustrated and anxious and immediately respond, "I can't."
2. They can't believe they are good, smart, handsome, pretty, or worthy of praise.
3. They often put down their own abilities.
4. Because they are insecure, they avoid trying new ideas or activities.
5. Their low self-esteem causes them to feel unloved and unwanted.
6. Rather than take the consequences when things go wrong, they blame other children and make excuses for their own actions.
7. They are easily influenced by other children.

## 7 Ways to Develop Self-Esteem

1. Take the stigma out of failure. No one is perfect. Remember to praise your child for a job well done or for a good effort on a hard task. Don't exaggerate, but be supportive. Say, "You almost made the team, and the coach said to be sure to try again next season."
2. Communicate your love. Your love is a genuine boost to your child's self-esteem. Hugs tell children their parents think they are terrific. Children who know their parents love them and are proud of them can tackle problems head on.
3. Learn when to let go and laugh and when to be firm. Have a reasonable discipline policy that allows you to ease up or set limits. Before acting, decide if disciplinary action is really necessary.
4. Accept the positive and negative feelings your child expresses. For instance, don't expect hugs from an angry child.
5. Be a good example of how to cope with frustration and disappointment. If you throw temper tantrums, expect to see the same behavior from your child.
6. Set reasonable expectations and be an active, sympathetic listener. Teach your child to know and accept her limitations and be tolerant of her mistakes.
7. Provide time for your kid to pursue his talents and interests without interference.[1]

## Sports and Self-Esteem

The discipline and cooperation children learn from participating in a sport will carry over to other activities. For example, the skills required to play baseball include running, throwing, catching, and concentration. The batter who fails to focus on a ball pitched to him will probably miss it. Here are eight questions to ask when considering how sports might benefit your child:

1. At what sports does my child excel?
2. What does my child like to do in her spare time?
3. What activities does he like? Does he prefer individual or team sports?
4. Is my child mature physically and emotionally?
5. Does she have good hand-eye coordination? What about her running speed, endurance, and strength?
6. Is teasing by other players or criticism by the coach a problem? If so, choose an individual sport.
7. Is self-discipline or concentration a problem? Consider karate or tae kwon do.
8. Can my child cope in group activities, or is he a loner? Consider soccer. It's a team sport that involves running and kicking, and even kids that lack coordination do okay.

## A Dream Comes True: Lessons from Adrienne Johnson

Imagine playing basketball on dirt courts and shooting at make-believe baskets or milk crates nailed to garages and utility poles. That's the way star WNBA basketball player Adrienne Johnson learned how to play the game she loves. Most of the kids in the Louisville, Kentucky, neighborhood where she grew up played basketball. Adrienne learned to dribble, pass, and shoot baskets by playing with her cousins, her friends, and almost anyone else willing to play with a girl. In the 2000 season she had these outstanding accomplishments:

- finished second in the voting for the WNBA Most Improved Player award
- averaged 13.6 points per game
- shot 89.5 percent at the free-throw line
- set a single-season record for three-point field goals (52)
- averaged 33.3 minutes of play per game

Use the following tips from Adrienne to encourage your child to succeed in the sport he or she enjoys. Adrienne Johnson played basketball almost her whole life, and she knows that hard work, discipline, and a right attitude count in basketball and in life. Here are her tips for children who love sports:

1. Keep trying. Don't give up even if you are cut from a team. Keep trying, because it may take four or five times before you make it.
2. Work on game fundamentals. To succeed, you must know the fundamentals of the game.
3. Develop a can-do attitude. Be willing to work hard to develop your abilities and talents.[2]

## How to Spot a Troubled Child

If you think your child may be struggling emotionally, consider some of the following questions:

1. Has your child stopped enjoying nearly all activities?
2. Does your child appear sad and constantly complain of being tired?
3. Does she cry for long periods but can't explain her tears?
4. Does your child become agitated or angry? Is he masking his depression with displays of anger?
5. Have you noticed a change in your child's eating habits or observed a significant weight loss or gain?
6. Are you worried about your child's sleeping habits? Does your child complain about sleepless nights? Or does he or she sleep excessively?
7. Is your child's thinking slow, confused, and indecisive?
8. Do your child's statements show feelings of worthlessness, excessive blame, or inappropriate guilt? Does she talk about death and suicide, or has she attempted suicide? (If so, get immediate help.)

## Clinical Depression

Blues that last for more than a couple of weeks may signal depression and should be discussed with a mental health specialist. Remember, if your child is depressed, it's not your fault. Depression is a disease that can be cured with treatment, and over time the majority of children improve.

### 11 Guidelines for Helping Depressed Kids

1. *Understand the cause and the symptoms of depression.* Even though the severely depressed child stares, turns away, or ignores greetings, he doesn't want to be that way, and he would rather be normal.
2. *Take even the hint of suicide very seriously.* Any talk about a hopeless future is a warning signal that the child is considering taking her life.
3. *Suggest that he tell you about his suicidal thoughts or plans.* It helps the suicidal person if the subject can be brought out into the open and discussed.
4. *Don't wait; get your depressed child to the family doctor.* She may be able to refer you to the right psychologist or psychiatrist. In case of emergency call the local police or the National Suicide Hot Line at 1-800-784-2433.
5. *Don't overreact, but support your child.* Make the entire family aware of your child's depression. Ask the family to be positive rather than to bring up the child's failures. Remember he can't do anything about the way he feels.
6. *Don't keep away from your depressed child.* She doesn't have the Bubonic plague, and she's not contagious. Isolation could make her feel worse and more alone.
7. *Grasp the fact that a depressed child really hurts.* It doesn't help to tell him to "get over it" or to say, "You're just imagining it."
8. *Don't use sympathy.* Sympathy will reinforce her depressed feelings of hopelessness. In most cases it is better to say,

"I'm aware or sensitive to the way you feel," than, "I know how you feel."

9. *Don't let him skip meals.* Say, "Even if you don't feel like eating, you must get something in your stomach." Starving won't lift his depression. Rather than nag your child about not eating, sit down and eat with him.

10. *Keep her active.* Don't ask, "What would you like to do?" If you are planning a shopping trip or going to work out at the gym, suggest that she come along. "I'm going to the gym now and I'd like you to help me with my workout." By getting her involved, you can help her break down her destructive habits.

11. *Make "no teasing" an indisputable rule in your family.* Rather, talk about the past accomplishments of your depressed child, and focus on things he can do. Try to rebuild a positive attitude about life.[3]

## When Your Child Cheats

Does your child put off studying for a coming test until it's too late? If you ask her about her homework, does she say something like, "It's okay, Mom, I know the stuff." Probably she thinks it's true until she reads the test questions, panics, and copies her neighbor's answers.

### Why Do Kids Cheat?

Experts say that cheating is out of control, but most kids will tell you that they know cheating is wrong. While there is really no good reason for cheating, understanding why children cheat can help parents begin to teach their kids to make better choices. There are probably as many excuses for cheating as there are kids who cheat, but the following is a list of the most common excuses kids give for cheating:

1. Kids cheat because they are afraid of what their parents will say and do. *You're grounded until your grades improve.*
2. Kids cheat because of the intense pressure to get good grades. *My teacher said if I want a scholarship I'd better get A's.*
3. All of their friends cheat. *She was cheating so I copied her paper.*
4. Kids cheat because they are overloaded with homework. *I'm so tired because I stayed up late doing my homework.*

## The Consequences of Cheating

Often the benefits of cheating seem to outweigh the negatives. That's why it is important to talk to your child about cheating before it becomes a problem. Some of the consequences of cheating are:

1. Cheating in school makes it easier to cheat later in life.
2. Cheating will cause a loss of respect by others.
3. Cheating is a lie and fools people into thinking you know more than you do.
4. Cheating isn't fair to the other kids.
5. Cheating isn't worth the consequences when you're caught.
6. If you're caught cheating, the teacher will never trust you again.
7. Cheating means you will lose your self-confidence.
8. If you cheat, your parents will find out and feel bad.

## What Parents Can Do

Parents must discuss cheating with their kids. Very young children don't understand what cheating is, but by the time they are in elementary school, they can understand the meaning of concepts like right, wrong, and fair. Explain what you expect from your child, and together review the school's policy on cheating.

1. Talk to your child's teacher about ways to help your child feel successful without cheating.
2. Don't ignore cheating. Have a discussion with your child before it becomes a serious problem.
3. Find out why your child cheats. If it is a personal problem, try to help him solve it. Also, discuss it with his teacher.
4. Let your child know that you are worried about her behavior but still love her.
5. Remember that you are an example to your child. If he sees you cheating in a game or at the store, he will think it is okay.
6. Make honesty a top priority in your home.[4]

# 7

# School Phobia

School is an exciting place, and most children hate to miss it. But for some children, the joy is replaced by an uncontrollable fear of school. School-phobic children sometimes develop mysterious illnesses. Other signals include tardiness, cut classes, unfinished homework assignments, and disrupted living patterns.

Experts say that fears, including school fear, are common among school-age children. The stronger the fear, the longer it will take to overcome it. Although living with school-phobic children is a challenge, most children either eventually outgrow it or learn to handle their fears.

## Questions to Consider about School Phobia

Do you think your child has school phobia? In a sentence or two, answer the following questions about your child's school behavior.

1. Have I talked to my child's teacher, and do I have a clear idea about the problem?

_____

_____

2. When did my child start to dread school? Is the fear related to a problem at recess or to a problem in the classroom, or does it include school in general?

_____

_____

3. What is your child's side of the story? Identify with her problems, and try to understand the way she feels.

_____

_____

4. Who else can I talk to? (Find an expert in child behavior and thoroughly discuss your child's problem. Begin with the school psychologist or school counselor.)

_____

_____

## Identify Fears

Kids sometimes have difficulty pinpointing and expressing fears. Here are some fears children of various ages experience as reported by mothers, psychologists, and teachers. Use the following list of fears as a guide to help you determine why your child is afraid to attend school.

1. Schoolyard or bus stop bullies
2. Scorn from his peers (for glasses, learning problems, etc.)
3. Being ignored by her peers
4. Teacher pressure (high expectations, overwhelming amounts of homework)
5. Unfamiliar or larger school
6. Male teacher (for young girls with no father figure)
7. Failure (tests, grades, own expectations)
8. Bus (not making it to the right stop)
9. Separation (afraid to be on own without a parent)
10. Inability to cope with new schedules (half-day schedule to full-day first grade, multiple teachers in junior high)[1]

## Examples of School Phobia

Psychiatrist Robert Spitzer relates the story of Billy, a child who refused to go to school. By the time Billy started second grade, his enchantment with learning was gone, and in its place was an immobilizing fear of school. Sometimes his feelings of dread were intolerable. On those days he took a smudged piece of paper out of his pocket and read what his mother had written: "You are not getting out of school early today. If you have to do your papers over and over again, please just do the best you can. Do not think about the time and it will go quickly. Mom."

Billy's fear of school forced him to carry the note each day. He was afraid that his parents would go someplace without him or a horrible accident would snatch them away from him. Without the note to reassure him, he would sneak away from his class and run home.

Tina's parents found out just how hard it is to force a child to go to school. According to Spitzer, a short time before Tina was supposed to leave for school, she surprised her mother by refusing to budge from the house. When her mother insisted, Tina hid in the basement and cried. The only way her mom could persuade her to leave the house was to promise to drive her to school and then stay with her for lunch. Tina went to fourth grade off and on for the next three months, but her behavior continued to slip. Finally, she refused to go to school unless her parents lifted her out of bed, dressed and fed her, placed her in the car, and drove to school.

A combination of events was responsible for Tina's fear. But a major ingredient was her belief that someone in her family was going to die while she was at school. For Tina, the easiest way to relieve her anxiety was to make sure nothing happened, so she refused to leave home.[2]

### Living with Pressure

The pressure to conform to peer group standards is strong, and some children hate school because of it. If your child avoids school because of pressure to conform to the values of other children, here's what to do.

1. *Get the facts.* Are one or two classmates causing the problem, or is it a larger group of children? Does it involve moral questions, appearances, behavior?
2. *Determine the severity of the problem.* Some problems disappear in a day or two without parental intervention.
3. *Be your child's advocate.* The problem may not seem serious to you, but it is to your child. Try to remember how you once worried about your clothes, about your looks, and about what kids said behind your back.
4. *Support your child's individuality and uniqueness.* Risking disapproval takes strength. Help your child realize he's special without conforming to other kid's standards.

## Shy Kids and School Phobia

Many shy children attend school more or less regularly but with great discomfort. These children tend to be highly anxious and lack the skills needed to handle social interactions, said Maureen Hogan in the *Nassau County Psychologist*.[3]

## Key Points for a Successful Return to School

Most experts agree that the first priority of parents should be to get their child through the school doors. At this point you must put aside your feelings and, if necessary, haul your kicking and screaming child into the building. However, before you try that, consider the suggestions of psychologists John and Helen Krumboltz.

A school counselor's use of the fear-reduction principle helped a frightened seventh grader master his fear of junior high school. He was having a difficult time because he missed the attention he received in a self contained elementary school classroom.

Shortly after school started in September, he began missing classes. His parents and the school counselor worked out a plan to improve his attendance and reduce his fear. First, he was told it was okay to go to the counselor's office and call his mom or dad if he became anxious. Next, to check on his attendance, the counselor asked his teachers to sign a memo that he had attended their classes. After each class he returned to the counselor's office, and the counselor walked with him to his next class.

Finally, at the end of the day he checked in with the counselor to talk about his day and plan the next day. In a short time he had conquered his fear of junior high and was enjoying school.[4]

They suggest that parents use the "fear reduction principle" to help their kids conquer school phobia. The principle goes like this: "To help children overcome their fears of a particular situation, gradually increase their exposure to the feared situation while they are otherwise comfortable, relaxed, and secure or rewarded."[5] The following is an example of the steps to a child's gradual return to school.

Day 1: Get your child up in the morning and dressed for school.

Day 2: Get your child dressed and drive her past the school to see what it is like.

Day 3: Sit in the classroom with your child for two periods.

Day 4: Insist that your child goes to school alone and stays until lunch.

Day 5: Your child returns to school for a full day of instruction.

## 11 Guidelines for the Stay-at-Home Child

1. If she stays home because of a stomachache, make her stay boring rather than fun. See that she is safe and comfortable. Include a structured routine with no TV or other privileges.
2. Play down conversations about his anxieties.
3. Don't discuss your youngster's feelings. Don't ask, "How do you feel this morning?" or "Do you want to go to school today?"
4. Inform your child that school attendance is expected and you won't accept anything else.
5. Ask the teacher for a conference that includes the school psychologist and other staff members who have contact with your child.

6. If physical symptoms are present, check with your family physician. A thorough medical assessment may be helpful.
7. If your child refuses to go to school for more than a week or if his refusal is chronic, check with your family physician. He may advise you to see a child psychologist or psychiatrist.
8. Be cautious about a change in school or class since new situations may intensify separation anxiety.
9. Any attempt to make school less demanding or easier probably will not help.
10. Consider home instruction as a last resort since it may reinforce school refusal.
11. Before beginning home instruction, discuss with your child the criteria for reentry into school.

## Understanding Your Child's School Phobia—A Quiz

The following quiz will help you understand the possible reasons your child resists going to school. It is based on the Revised Manifest Anxiety Scale published by Western Psychological Services.

Check the statements that best describe your child's anxiety.

|  | Yes | No |
|---|---|---|
| 1. Most of the time my child can't make up his mind. | ___ | ___ |
| 2. My child often loses his temper. | ___ | ___ |
| 3. My child won't go to sleep unless I hold her hand. | ___ | ___ |
| 4. He or she sometimes trembles or shakes. | ___ | ___ |
| 5. He sometimes wakes up scared. | ___ | ___ |
| 6. He or she has bad dreams or nightmares. | ___ | ___ |
| 7. She is deathly afraid of spiders. | ___ | ___ |
| 8. He worries about what others think about him. | ___ | ___ |
| 9. She worries about what her parents will say to her. | ___ | ___ |
| 10. My child's feelings get hurt easily. | ___ | ___ |

|                                                              | Yes | No |
|--------------------------------------------------------------|-----|----|
| 11. My child often has intense periods of fear.              | ___ | ___ |
| 12. He is afraid something terrible will happen to his parents. | ___ | ___ |
| 13. She worries that her parents will have a bad accident.   | ___ | ___ |
| 14. He thinks he is going crazy.                             | ___ | ___ |
| 15. My child believes that he can't do things as well as others. | ___ | ___ |
| 16. He is afraid of almost everything.                       | ___ | ___ |
| 17. My child thinks that others do not like what he does.    | ___ | ___ |
| 18. My child feels alone even when others are around.        | ___ | ___ |
| 19. She believes that other children are happier.            | ___ | ___ |
| 20. He thinks someone will say he does it the wrong way.     | ___ | ___ |
| 21. She says it's hard to think about schoolwork.            | ___ | ___ |
| 22. He wiggles in his seat.                                  | ___ | ___ |
| 23. My child is tired a lot.                                 | ___ | ___ |
| 24. His heartbeat sometimes races or pounds.                 | ___ | ___ |
| 25. My child complains that she is dizzy or lightheaded.     | ___ | ___ |
| **Total**                                                    | ___ | ___ |

This quiz should be interpreted cautiously. The "Yes" statements may help you understand your child's anxiety about school. If the majority of the responses are in the "Yes" column, consider discussing your child's behavior with a child psychologist or psychiatrist.

## What Parents and Children Say about School Fear

Use the following examples and questions to consider how you might handle school fear in your child at different ages.

### A Preschool Parent

"I have a four-year-old daughter who started preschool this year. She has been in school for about five months now, and she still cries, clings on to me, and vomits every morning I drop her off at school. Everyone tells me that children usually adjust to school after a few weeks, but in my daughter's case, it seems like the first day of school every day. I just keep at it, and I hope that one day she will be happy. I am getting very tired of it. Her teachers are also getting tired of it. What shall I do?"

What advice would you give this parent?

(a) Continue to drop her off at school each day.
(b) Tell the teacher to do the best she can.
(c) Observe her class and check out her behavior during the school day.
(d) Consider enrolling her in a small, home-style preschool with three to five children since she may not be ready for larger school classes.

**Answer:** Item (d) is the best answer.

Additional ideas:

_____

_____

_____

### A Middle School Parent

"Sometimes I think I'm the only person with a child who has school phobia. I have a thirteen-year-old son who is not in school currently. This is the third year we have gone through his refusing to go to school. He is on medication and sees both a psychologist and a psychiatrist. We are in the process of setting him up with a tutor. I feel like this will never end."

With the information you have, what advice would you give this parent?

(a) Stop spending money on psychologists and psychiatrists.
(b) Force him to go to school. Drag him through the door if you must.
(c) Get his side of the story.
(d) Continue with the tutor.

**Answer:** Item (b) is the correct answer. Remember, most experts agree that the first priority of parents should be to get their child through the school doors. At this point you must put aside your feelings and, if necessary, haul your kicking and screaming child into the building.

Additional ideas:

_____

_____

_____

### *"I Have School Phobia"—A Teenager's Story*

"I'm seventeen and I have school phobia. I am halfway through my senior year, but I am sure I have missed too many days to pass. I think of any excuse I can not to go to school. I have really bad separation anxiety. I don't see a psychologist or anyone like that. My mom refuses. She just can't understand why I won't go to school. I have always cried and begged for my mom to not send me to school. I have always been the girl who never comes to school. I have pretty good grades when I go to school, but it is so hard. Teachers sure don't understand."

What would you advise this child to do?

(a) Talk to the school psychologist or school counselor about her school fear.
(b) Drop out of school and find a full-time job.

(c) Study for the GED (General Education Development test) and earn her high school equivalency certificate.

**Answer:** Item (a) is the best solution for this student.

Additional ideas:

_____

_____

_____

## Spiritual Approaches to School Phobia

Facing the problem head-on should help diminish a child's fear of school. Darlene Hoffa writes about specific prayer in her book *What Do I Say When I Pray?* She recommends that we talk to God in detail about every part of our lives. Children understand prayer that is directed to a need, and they can use this kind of prayer to handle their fears about school.

### Spiritual Comfort for a Frightened Child

1. Fear does not come from God (see Rom. 8:15).
2. Jesus loves children and doesn't want them to be anxious or fearful about anything (see Mark 10:13–16; Phil. 4:6).
3. When we ask, God gives peace instead of fear (see Phil. 4:5–7).

### A Child's Specific Prayer List

You can help your child make a specific prayer list by putting down on paper the problem, his hurt feelings, and the goal of the prayer. The specific prayer list of a child who is afraid his classmate will beat him up might look like this:

103

1. Pray that God will protect him.
2. Pray that he will be happy in school.
3. Pray that the other boy won't hurt him.
4. Pray that they will become friends.
5. Pray for new friends.

# 8

# Take Charge of Your ADHD Child

How much do you know about Attention Deficit Hyper-activity Disorder (ADHD)? Below are five scenarios that describe children with ADHD. Each scene has several possible endings. Choose the ending that you think is the best description of an ADHD child.

1. You lose your temper when your ten-year-old doesn't re-member the two or three things you asked him to buy at the supermarket. A ten-year-old who claims he can't remember directions
   (a) is faking it
   (b) pays less attention to directions than other children
   (c) can't tune out the distractions around him

If you chose (c), your answer is correct. ADHD children can't ignore the whispers of schoolmates, the movement of the second hand on the wall clock, or a weird shadow. It is like listening to a radio with poor reception: ADHD children can't tune out the interference.

2. Instead of making her bed, Diane stares at the wall. Her teacher complains that Diane daydreams at school too. Her problem
   (a) is something other than ADHD, because daydreaming is not a symptom of ADHD
   (b) may be ADHD, since daydreaming is a symptom of an attention problem

If your answer is (b), you're doing great. Some ADHD children have attention problems but are not hyperactive. Daydreaming is a normal behavior, but it also may be a symptom of ADHD. For some children it indicates their inability to focus on a task. And then the impulse to chase butterflies or trap a creepy insect in a jar overrules finishing the job you have assigned him.

3. At the family reunion Josh ran through the house chasing his cousins. And when the family ate dinner, he grabbed the dessert. His mom was a nervous wreck. "He's just like his dad," his grandma said. He behaves like his dad because ADHD
   (a) is a disease he inherited from his dad
   (b) is a neurodevelopmental disorder
   (c) is a neurodevelopmental disorder with a genetic connection

The correct answer is (c). ADHD is "neuro" because it affects the brain, and it is "developmental" because the way it affects behavior depends on the person's age. And it has a genetic connection—in fact, some experts estimate that 40 percent of ADHD children have a parent with a neurodevelopmental disorder and 35 percent have a sibling with the problem.

4. When your ADHD child threw a temper tantrum at the supermarket, a neighbor scowled and muttered, "What that kid needs is a good swat on his bottom." She was
   (a) right because parenting without structure or discipline causes ADHD
   (b) right, and you know you are bad parents
   (c) wrong; physical discipline will not make ADHD go away

I hope your answer is (c), because there are better ways to discipline an ADHD child than spanking. Effective discipline methods include time-outs, loss of privileges, and having to face the natural consequences for unacceptable behavior.

5. Mary and Josh worry because their toddler doesn't listen or follow instructions. Her behavior
   (a) means she is developing ADHD
   (b) is a problem now, but she probably will improve by kindergarten

Is your answer (b)? That's correct because nearly half the preschoolers considered to be potential ADHD children outgrow the behavior. Short attention span and poor impulse control are typical toddler behaviors. Research shows that there is at least a 40 percent chance that hyperactive, inattentive, impulsive toddlers will outgrow this behavior by the time they enter kindergarten. But there are some warning signs. Characteristics that predict the continuation of ADHD into later childhood include overactivity, inattention, negative mood, and low adaptability.

## ADHD: A Common Disorder

Experts estimate that 3 to 5 percent of children suffer from Attention Deficit Hyperactivity Disorder (ADHD), and boys are afflicted five to seven times more often than girls. ADHD behavior ranges from mild to extreme hyper-activity, impulsivity, and inattention. The disorder may go unrecognized until the child enters school, when telltale signs like fidgeting, poor concentration, and impulsiveness surface. The disorder affects school performance and peer relationships, and ADHD does not disappear as the child matures.

### Morning Madness: A Parent's View of ADHD

School day mornings are often frantic when parents and children need to get going early. But in families with children who have ADHD, the usual morning madness may be magnified tenfold. Children with ADHD forget where they put their homework or gym shoes, dawdle over getting dressed, tie up the bathroom, and take what seems like forever to eat breakfast, says Rebecca Kajander in her booklet *A Parent's View of ADHD*. She offers the following guidelines to help eliminate "before school madness":

1. Allow enough time in the morning to complete necessary tasks.
2. Establish a list of things to do. Place them in a set order and insist that they be completed in that order.
3. Develop a reward system for tasks completed on time and without a hassle.
4. Establish a time for homework and stick to it.
5. List the ways your child can succeed. For example, can he do five arithmetic problems instead of ten?
6. Do whatever it takes. Use a computer, flash cards, or games—anything that helps your child learn.[1]

### A Child's View of ADHD

For some school-age kids, school stops being fun shortly after the school day begins. And their day is crammed with complaints and demands such as *Can't you pay attention?*

*Don't you know where you put your lunch money?* and *Don't interrupt.* It's not that they don't try at school, but sometimes they can't remember directions or assignments. Here are nine tips to keep your ADHD child out of trouble:

1. Be explicit with your directions about school behavior and homework.
2. Restate directions if necessary.
3. Ask your child to paraphrase what you have said.
4. Depending on your child's age, find a sport or physical activity that he or she enjoys.
5. Push for a strong physical education program at school.
6. Together set daily behavioral goals that you agree your child can reach.
7. Encourage her to use a notebook to write down assignments.
8. Create a graphic homework organizer.
9. Develop a homework spreadsheet that will help your child organize and monitor assignments.

## 5 Key Points about ADHD

1. Many children outgrow what appear to be ADHD symptoms.
2. Diagnosing ADHD is difficult and controversial, especially in young children.
3. It's unfair to blame the parents of ADHD children for their child's behavior.
4. ADHD is not a disability that disappears in a few years.
5. Some estimate that 40 percent of ADHD children have a parent with the trait and 35 percent have a sibling with the problem.

## 5 Telltale Signs of ADHD

The onset of the following behaviors must be before the age of seven to indicate ADHD.

1. *Delayed visual motor skills.* Lack of small or large muscle coordination or sloppy, messy seatwork is an indicator of ADHD.
2. *Accident prone.* Often engages in physically dangerous activities without thinking about the outcome. ADHD kids tend to break an arm or leg, skin their knees, fall off of equipment, and visit the school nurse more often than non-ADHD children.
3. *Trouble getting along.* Often other kids dislike ADHD kids because they have trouble taking turns, sharing, and respecting the rights of others.
4. *Poor classroom behavior.* He or she doesn't seem to listen to instructions. Blurts out answers before the teacher has finished her statement. Loses things necessary to complete assignments and classroom tasks.
5. *Turns off in the middle of instructions.* Her short attention span results in shifts from one uncompleted task to another. The child is easily distracted by what goes on in the classroom.

## 13 Symptoms of ADHD

### Impulsivity

1. Butts into conversations or games
2. Can't wait his turn
3. Has trouble playing quietly
4. Talks excessively

### Inattention

5. Makes careless mistakes in schoolwork or other activities
6. Does not seem to listen when spoken to directly
7. Easily distracted
8. Doesn't follow through on tasks
9. Often forgets daily activities

### Hyperactivity

10. Often fidgets and squirms

11. Leaves his seat in the classroom when expected to stay seated
12. Has trouble playing quietly
13. Talks excessively

### 4 Myths about ADHD

Several myths about ADHD may be confusing you. Here are some of the most widely believed myths about ADHD.

1. Sugar causes ADHD. Not a single scientific study shows a relationship between sugar intake and the hyperactive behavior of children.
2. There is a significant link between thyroid functioning and hyperactivity. And hormones have been shown to have a connection to ADHD. This has not been proven to be true.
3. Fluorescent lighting gives off certain soft x-rays and radio frequencies that cause children to become hyperactive. Now no one takes this seriously.
4. Motion sickness is connected to the brain's vestibular system, which regulates energy levels, sense of balance, and

### Research: A Genetic Connection

Dr. Russell Barkley says in his book *Taking Charge of ADHD*, "So far studies indicate a very strong genetic contribution to ADHD. Everything we know points to the idea that children with ADHD have less brain activity in the frontal regions, precisely those brain centers known to be involved in behavioral inhibition, persistence of responding, resistance to distraction, and controlling one's activity. The precise cause of this underactivity is not known, but lower levels of several brain chemicals in this region may be the root of the problem."[2]

gravity. According to this theory, any impairment in this system can lead to hyperactivity and impulsive behavior. Proponents of this theory recommend that children with ADHD or learning problems take over-the-counter motion sickness medication. This theory is inconsistent with what is known about hyperactivity.[3]

## Probable Causes of ADHD

1. Brain injury or abnormal brain development caused by trauma, disease, exposure to alcohol and tobacco, and early exposure to high levels of lead may cause ADHD.
2. Diminished activity in certain brain regions—children with ADHD have a lower level of brain activity than non-ADHD children.
3. If parents have ADHD, their children are likely to have ADHD too.[4]

## Finding a Quality Doctor

Psychologist Richard Barkley recommends that "any child who is to be evaluated for ADHD should first have a standard pediatric exam to rule out medical causes of the symptoms."[5] Furthermore, if there are medical problems such as seizures, you may want to consult a pediatrician or neurologist, says Barkley. Here are eight tips to help you choose an ADHD professional:

1. Check with a local ADHD parent group.
2. If there isn't a support group in your area, check online to see if there is a practitioner in your area.
3. Contact professional organizations such as the American Medical Association or American Psychological Association to see if the practitioner you select is licensed.
4. Ask other parents for their recommendation.
5. Ask your department of health if they have a referral service.

6. Find out if there are any malpractice complaints filed against the practitioner.
7. Ask where the practitioner received her professional training and if she regularly treats ADHD children.
8. Ask if the practitioner considers himself well trained. As Barkley says, "Don't be embarrassed to ask the doctor or other professional direct questions. The professional to call is the one in your area who seems to know the most about ADHD. Find another professional if the one you ask is offended by what you ask."[6]

## Why Use Medication?

For most parents the combination of children and medication is scary. They may have heard rumors that a child's personality changes with ADHD medication and that it will stunt his growth. On the other hand, research shows that behavior improves in about 80 percent of the children placed on medication.

Medications like Ritalin may have a calming effect on the child's behavior and increase her ability to handle frustration, follow directions, and complete tasks and assignments.

But is medication safe? Ritalin has been used and studied since the 1940s. Like most drugs, it has side effects, but they have been shown to be easily managed. Side effects include loss of appetite, sleep disturbance, mild headaches and stomachaches, and irritability.

### 7 Questions to Ask the Doctor about ADHD Medication

1. What are the effects and the side effects of the medication?
2. How often should I give it to my child?
3. How often will you see my child to reevaluate the medication?
4. Is there any food or drink I should cut out of his diet?

5. If he accidentally takes an overdose of medication, what should I do?
6. May I have a fact sheet telling about this medication?
7. When should I stop giving him the medication?

## Medications Available to Treat ADHD

About 70 percent of children diagnosed as ADHD take some form of medication. Use the following chart to help you understand several of the leading drugs for hyperactive children. It is not a comprehensive list, and other medications may be prescribed for your child. Always follow your doctor's directions exactly.

| Name | Advantages | Dosage | Duration | Side Effects | Cautions |
|---|---|---|---|---|---|
| Ritalin | Works quickly | Tablet, 2–3 times a day | 3–4 hours | Trouble sleeping, decreased appetite, weight loss, headache | Not for child with high anxiety or motor tics |
| Dexedrine | Works in 30–60 minutes | Tablet, capsule, or liquid, 2–3 times a day | 3–4 hours | See above | See above |
| Cylert | Chewable tablet | Tablet, once daily | 12–24 hours | See above | See above |
| Tofranil | Helps children who also have depression or anxiety | Tablet, 1–2 times a day | 12–24 hours | Dry mouth, poor appetite, dizziness, mild to rapid heart rate, constipation | May take 2–8 weeks for response; regular blood tests to check liver function |
| Catapres | Helps children/teens with tic disorder or severe hyperactivity and/or aggression | Tablet, 2–4 times a day; or patch on skin | Tablet, 3–6 hours; patch on skin changed 1–2 times a week | Drowsiness, low blood pressure, stomachache, dry mouth | Sudden stop of medication could cause increase in blood pressure |

## How to Help Your ADHD Child Succeed

Do you wonder if you are to blame for your ADHD child's weird behavior? ADHD is not a disability that disappears in a few years. And psychologists say that a battery of screening tests, observation, and interviews are necessary before a child can be labeled ADHD. It's unfair to blame the parents for their child's behavior. But parents can watch for signs of an ADHD disorder.

The number of children being diagnosed as ADHD is increasing. Yet diagnosing ADHD is difficult and controversial, especially in young children. Symptoms vary in degree and severity. In the following sections we will look at some common behavior problems of ADHD children and how parents can help.

"My mother didn't take me to the church nursery or send me to Sunday school because she was too embarrassed by my 'wild behavior.' Rumor had it at church that I was 'retarded' and my parents were keeping me home in hiding. I drove the teacher in my one-room schoolhouse classroom to distraction with my constant interruptions and hyperactivity. . . . I talked and moved nonstop, often running wildly in circles, pretending to be a horse, until the day I smacked into a corner and collapsed on the floor sobbing as blood gushed out of my head. My mother was always in tears over the things I ruined. My home was organized and structured. Expectations were high and nonsense was not tolerated. Today, I might be diagnosed as having ADHD."[7]

Elaine McEwan, *Attention Deficit Disorder*

## What Would You Do?

Parenting Jack is exhausting. His mom wants to believe that her son will grow out of it, but year after year the struggle continues. Each school year Jack's teachers comment about his inattention, his disruptive behavior, and the time it takes for him to finish even the simplest task. Finally, a team of specialists including a psychologist meet with his parents. They say that Jack has Attention Deficit Hyperactivity Disorder (ADHD) and he'll do better in a special class. But it still takes him forever to finish the simplest tasks, and getting him to school on time often seems impossible.

Have you experienced similar problems? How would you advise Jack's mom about each of the following issues?

His school behavior: _____

_____

Placing him in a special education class: _____

_____

Getting him to school on time: _____

_____

Improving his behavior at home: _____

_____

There are no simple answers to children's ADHD behavior. If you aren't satisfied with the answers you have been given, continue to seek help for your child.

## *Winning the Homework Battle*

By the end of the school day, ADHD children probably feel exhausted from trying to cope at school, and homework is more than they can handle. Homework hassles can be avoided, at least most of the time. Here are eight ways to help your child complete his homework without a battle.

1. Set a timer for the length of time the assignments should take. Agree on a reward for completion in the allotted time.
2. Have a regular work space nearby where you can check on his progress. If you can't find a quiet corner for a desk or table, use a large box that can be stored between sessions.
3. If your child finds background music soothing, play it during the homework session. Turn off the TV and anything else that might distract him from his assignments.
4. Don't forget to give praise for even the smallest accomplishment.
5. Create a homework folder. Purchase a two-pocket folder to hold materials coming home from school and completed work going back to school.
6. Ask the teacher for a copy of the weekly assignments, and staple it on the outside of the folder.
7. Inside the folder, label one of the pockets "work to be completed" and the other pocket "completed work."
8. Give your child a sticker if she completes her homework assignment on time. Set the number of stickers required before you reward your child. The goal is to have all assignments completed on time.

## *Setting Effective Goals*

Strive to set reachable, practical goals for your ADHD child. Try the following ways to set clear-cut goals.

## Parents' Report

"Monica Kingston says that when Danny comes home from school his medication has pretty well worn off, and if his homework isn't done by dinner he is shot for the day. The Scotts experience a similar situation with Billy: When the Ritalin wears off around 5:00 p.m. and can't be repeated, we have real problems with homework," writes Elaine McEwan.[8]

1. Establish clear, consistent rules of behavior. ADHD kids need to know the exact behaviors that are expected from them and the consequences for misbehavior.
2. Develop a discipline system that works. It should reward appropriate behavior and include consequences for inappropriate behavior.
3. Set up a behavior modification plan to change intolerable behavior at home and in the classroom. The plan should include rewards that are valuable to your child.
4. Develop a daily schedule that doesn't vary. Post a daily and weekly schedule on the fridge or bulletin board where your child can check her day's activities and responsibilities.
5. Organize the daily items he needs. There should be a place for everything and everything should be kept in its place. Then if he needs an item, he will know exactly where to find it. This includes things like his backpack, clothing, supplies, and sports equipment.
6. Stress how important it is that your child writes down her assignments and brings home the needed books.

### Managing Distractions

Have you ever said to your child, "How many times do I have to tell you＿＿＿＿？" Paying attention is something

ADHD kids just can't do as well as non-ADHD ones. This inability constantly gets them in trouble at school. More than a hundred studies have measured the attention span of ADHD children. The majority of the studies showed that children with ADHD spent less time paying attention to what they were asked to do than children who did not have ADHD. This boils down to the fact that the inattentive child is easily distracted by movement, noises, smell, or colors, and he or she may daydream too.

### How to Cut Down on At-Home Distractions

1. If your meals are chaotic and the dining room table is near a window, close the curtains.
2. Give directions one at a time. Be clear about what you want, and wait until you're satisfied with the result before you give another direction.
3. If necessary, say it again. Stay calm and restate your request. Train your child to say, "Please stop, Mom. I'm getting confused and I need you to say it again."
4. Show, don't tell. When you give directions, you may have to show him what to do or use a chart to remind him of his tasks.
5. Break a complex job into smaller parts. Instead of telling her to clean her room, say, "First empty the wastebasket, then pick up your toys."
6. Reward progress. Don't expect perfection, but reward the small gains.

### Establishing a Daily Routine

Without a doubt, ADHD kids can cause unbelievable disorder in their classrooms and homes. Checklists are useful because the child must refer to the list rather than relying on his parent to repeat instructions. When you make up a checklist, be sure that what you require is not asking more than your child can deliver. If the list is overloaded with items, your child may lose interest and simply ignore the whole list.

### 7 Tips for Chaos-Free Routines

If you want to reduce chaos (and who doesn't?), use the following tips to establish routines at home.

1. Don't overload your child's checklist with too many items. Most checklists range between three and eight items.
2. Keep the list's expectations clear and stated in terms that both the parent and child understand. For example, an after-school chart might read: "(1) Change your clothes. (2) Eat the snack in the refrigerator. (3) Do your homework. (4) Watch TV."
3. Use a calendar to plan family events. If it's not on the calendar, it's not happening.
4. Use a timer to help your child complete a task. Children like to race against time and win.
5. Use red and green colored dots available at office supply stores to mark a bedroom or bathroom "okay to enter" (green) or "off-limits" (red).
6. Use incentives (rewards) to reinforce tasks completed to your satisfaction.
7. Make picture lists for younger children or children with reading problems. Pictures of a bed, breakfast, clothing, and books will get the point across.

### Improving Social Skills

As a parent of an ADHD child, you can be almost certain that your child's school career will be marred by fighting and arguing with other children. She may alienate her peers by refusing to share, take turns, or respect other children's point of view.

According to Elaine McEwan, half of all children with ADHD are likely to experience difficulty making and keeping friends. Their lack of awareness of social cues results in immature play and social interests. Plus, ADHD children have little regard for the social consequences of their behavior.[9]

### 7 Steps to Better Social Skills

1. Invite one friend at a time to play with your ADHD child. If more than one friend comes over, your child probably won't have much fun. Quiet play with one other child is less stressful than group play.
2. Talk over family rules. Before the friend arrives, talk about the kind of behavior you expect from your child. Then check to see that the rules for play are being followed.
3. Let your child decide on the toys he will share. Talk to him about the toys he is willing to share with a friend and the special toys that he wants to keep for himself. Put away the toys he decides not to share.
4. Role-play behavior in different social situations. Work on one situation at a time. Practice the correct way to wait in line, behave in the cafeteria, and ride on the school bus.
5. Talk over problems. Role-play ways to avoid problems that may occur in different social situations.
6. Try short play periods. When a friend is invited over, limit play time to an hour or two. Plan a reward if all goes well.
7. Don't criticize her in front of others. Correction of inappropriate behavior is okay, but don't embarrass her in front of a friend. It's better to end the play early and send the playmate home. Then calmly explain what went wrong.

# 9

# All about Special Education

If you have a child with special needs, one word you will hear regarding his education is "inclusion." Special education changed with the passage of the Individuals with Disabilities Education Act (IDEA) in 1973 and its 1997 amendments. This landmark legislation moved children with special needs from segregated classrooms into regular classrooms.

"The problem with segregated special education is that children will not learn to live in a non-disabled world. Kids in a segregated class will think that emotionally disturbed is the normal thing," said Art Shapiro, Kean University professor of special education, in the article "Special Education Inclusion: Making It Work."[1]

To make the law work, schools are required to have an Individualized Education Program (IEP) for each special needs kid. Each child's IEP includes an educational plan designed to meet his or her unique needs; it must be a plan that can be carried out in the regular classroom. As a result, many school districts' special education children have moved from segregated classrooms into regular classrooms.

## Eligibility for Special Education

Federal law mandates that every child will receive a free and appropriate education in the least restrictive environment possible. This means that children with special needs have the right to receive special services or accommodations through the public schools. However, eligibility criteria and the procedures for implementing federal laws vary from state to state.

### 11 Qualifying Conditions

A child with any of the following disabilities qualifies for special education placement with related services.

1. *Orthopedic disabilities.* Severe orthopedic impairments or irregularities caused by diseases such as poliomyelitis or cerebral palsy; bone tuberculosis or amputations; or fractures or burns that cause tightening of a muscle, a tendon, or the skin resulting in deformity.
2. *Cognitive disabilities.* Low intellectual functioning in a child's early development plus defects of adaptive behavior.
3. *Speech or language impairments.* Communication difficulties that include receptive or expressive language skills; they may include stuttering and language difficulties involving structure, content, and processing skills.
4. *Traumatic brain injuries.* Head injuries resulting in impairment in cognition, speech and language, memory, attention reasoning, abstract reasoning, and more.
5. *Other health impairments.* Limited strength, vitality, or alertness due to chronic or acute health problems including a heart condition, tuberculosis, rheumatic fever, asthma, sickle-cell anemia, hemophilia, and epilepsy.

6. *Significant developmental delays.* Significant delayed cognitive, communication, social-emotional, or adaptive development experiences by children three to five years old.
7. *Learning disabilities.* Average or above average intellectual ability but unique learning problems that interfere with the ability to read write, spell, or learn arithmetic skills.
8. *Hearing impairments.* Hearing loss that prevents successful functioning in an educational program without specialized instruction, additional support services, and guidance.
9. *Autism.* A developmental disability that affects a child's social interaction and verbal and nonverbal communication; it is often evident before age three and adversely affects learning and educational performance.
10. *Emotional disturbances.* Social, emotional, or behavioral functioning that significantly interferes with the total educational program and development; the condition must be severe, chronic, and observable at school.
11. *Visual impairments.* Impairments, determined by an ophthalmologist, that are severe enough to prevent successful functioning in an educational program without guidance and accommodation.[2]

## Your Child's Educational Rights

All parents should be familiar with Section 504 of the Rehabilitation Act of 1973. It requires that schools do not discriminate against disabled children and do provide them with reasonable adjustments. It covers all private or public programs or activities that receive federal assistance. Under Section 504, any person who has an impairment that substantially limits a major life activity is considered disabled. Learning and social development are included under the list of major life activities. Usually these children's disabilities are less severe or do not fit with the IDEA criteria.

## 7 Reasonable Adjustments for a Disabled Child in a Regular Classroom

1. Untimed tests
2. Seat in the front of the class
3. Modified homework
4. Provision of the necessary services (speech, reading, psychological)
5. An amplifier on a hard-of-hearing child's desk
6. A clean change of clothes
7. An interpreter for non-English-speaking children

## 14 Rights of Parents Who Have Children with Special Needs

1. *You must be fully informed.* The school must inform you about all of the rights provided to you and your child under the law.
2. *You have the right to a free, appropriate public school education.* This means that your disabled child's education will be at no cost to you, and it will meet your child's special needs.
3. *You must be notified if the school wishes to evaluate your child.* Your permission is required for all special education services or changes in his or her placement.
4. *You may request an evaluation.* If you think your child needs special education or related services, take the following steps:
   a. Meet with your child's teacher to share your concerns and request an evaluation by the school's child-study team.
   b. Request evaluations and services in writing; date the copy.
   c. Always keep a copy for your records, including teacher observations, notes, and letters between home and school.
   d. Request independent professional evaluations (psychological, educational, speech, medical).
5. *You must give your informed consent.* You must understand and agree in writing to the evaluation and educational

program suggested for your child. You may withdraw your consent at any time.

6. *You may obtain an independent evaluation.* If you disagree with the outcome of the school's evaluation, you may request an independent evaluation.

7. *You have the right to appeal the conclusions and determination of the school's evaluation team.* The school is required to provide you with information about how to make an appeal.

8. *You may request a reevaluation.* Your child's educational program must be reviewed at least once during each calendar year, and the school must reevaluate your child at least every three years. However, if you think your child's current educational placement is no longer appropriate, ask for a reevaluation.

9. *You may have your child tested in the language he or she knows best.* If English is a second language for your child, request that all evaluations be completed in his or her native language.

10. *You may review all of your child's records and obtain free copies of these records.* If the information in your child's records is inaccurate, misleading, or violates the privacy or other rights of your child, you may ask that the information be changed. If the school refuses your request, you have the right to a hearing, and if that demand is refused, you may file a complaint with your state educational agency.

11. *You may participate in the development of your child's Individualized Education Program (IEP).* If the child is younger than four years old, an Individualized Family Service Plan (IFSP) is developed. The school must make every possible effort to notify you of the IEP or IFSP meeting and to arrange the meeting at a time and place that is convenient for both you and the school. You may participate in the decisions including your child's placement.

12. *You may have your child educated in the least restrictive school setting possible.* The school should make every effort to develop an educational program that will provide your

child with the services and supports needed in order to be taught with children who do not have disabilities.

13. *You may request a due process hearing or voluntary mediation to resolve differences with the school that can't be resolved informally.* Make your request in writing, date your request, and keep a copy for your records.

14. *You should be kept informed about your child's progress at least as often as parents of children who do not have disabilities.*[3]

## Always Be Your Child's Advocate

Children with special needs are guaranteed rights to services in school under federal and state laws. Parents should always speak for their child. The process, however, can be confusing and intimidating for parents. Here are five tips for advocating for your child.

1. Don't hesitate to take the necessary steps to make sure your child receives appropriate services.

2. Request copies of the school district's Section 504 plan. This is especially important when a school district refuses services.

3. If the school district does not respond to your request, you can contact a regional office of the U.S. Department of Education's Office of Civil Rights for assistance.

4. If the school district refuses services under the IDEA or Section 504 or both, challenge this decision through a due process hearing.

5. You may also need to retain your own attorney if you decide to appeal a school's decision.

## 12 Services Available to Children

1. An audiologist's services to diagnose and treat hearing defects. The service includes hearing evaluations, auditory training, speech reading, and speech conservation.

2. Counseling provided by psychologists, social workers, guidance counselors, or other qualified personnel.
3. Early identification and implementation of a plan for identifying a disability as early as possible in a child's life.
4. Medical services that determine a child's need for special education and related services.
5. Occupational therapy to improve the child's ability to perform tasks for independent functioning and prevent initial or further impairment or loss of functions.
6. Blind and visually impaired services to help those students move safely within their environments.
7. Parent counseling and training to help parents understand the special needs of their child and provide them with information about child development.
8. Physical therapy provided by a qualified physical therapist.
9. Psychological services that include the administration and interpretation of psychological tests. The psychologist consults with staff members to plan school programs that meet the special needs of the child.
10. School health services provided by a school nurse or other qualified person.
11. Speech and language services to identify children with speech or language problems and provide speech and language therapy.
12. Transportation to move the child to and from school and provide the specialized equipment required for a child with a disability.

## Special Education Placement

If you or your child's teacher thinks your child may need special education services, it is important that you understand the placement process and your options.

## 10 Steps to Special Education Placement

**Step 1:** Needs identified. This step includes locating, identifying, and evaluating children with disabilities. Parents may ask for their child to be evaluated for special education placement, or the referral may be made by the child's teacher.

**Step 2:** Evaluation made. A special education evaluation must include all areas of the suspected disability. Then a decision about an appropriate educational program will be made.

**Step 3:** Eligibility established. A group of qualified professionals will study the evaluation results to decide if your child has a disability. Parents may challenge the decision if they disagree with it.

**Step 4:** If the child is determined to be eligible for services, an Individualized Education Program (IEP) must be written for the child.

**Step 5:** IEP meeting scheduled. The school system must schedule and conduct an IEP meeting at a time convenient for parents. Parents must be notified early enough so that they can make arrangements to attend. The meeting will be held at a time and place agreeable to the parents and school. Parents will be told the purpose, time, location, and school staff who will be attending.

**Step 6:** IEP meeting is held and the IEP is written. The IEP team discusses the child's needs and writes the education plan. The parents must be included, and the student may attend when appropriate. If parents disagree with the placement, they can discuss their concerns with the IEP team members, or they can ask for mediation.

**Step 7:** Services are provided. The IEP is carried out as written. Parents are given a copy, and the child's teacher and service providers have access to the IEP.

**Step 8:** Progress is reported to the parents. The child's parents are regularly informed of their child's progress toward the completion of the yearly goals.

**Step 9:** The IEP is reviewed. The IEP team reviews the child's IEP at least once a year unless the parent requests additional reviews. Options include additional testing and an independent evaluation and mediation.

**Step 10:** Child is reevaluated. Reevaluations must be scheduled at least every three years, or more often if the parent or teacher requests it.

### 3 Useful Definitions

1. *Mainstreaming* usually refers to a special education student's placement in a regular classroom for one or more periods. The opportunity for this placement is earned by students who have shown the ability to keep up with the assigned work in a regular class.
2. *Inclusion* expresses the school's commitment to educate each child in a regular classroom to the maximum extent of his or her ability. If support services are necessary, they are brought to the student's class rather than the student traveling to another room for special services. This placement requires only that the child will benefit from such a placement.
3. *Full inclusion* means that regardless of the handicap or its severity, all handicapped students will be in a regular classroom program full time. All services will be brought to the child.

### 6 Questions and Answers about Special Education

If your child is having behavior problems plus academic problems, there is a good chance that he or she will be referred to a school psychologist for testing. The following are some of the questions that parents ask about testing and the answers to their questions.

**1. What kind of tests will be given to my child?**

Usually, the psychologist will give your child a battery of tests. These include achievement, intelligence, social and emotional, adjustment, and visual motor skill tests.

**2. Who else will be involved?**

If your child has a learning disability or is emotionally disturbed, a team of specialists will evaluate his problem. This team will include a psychologist, a reading specialist, a speech therapist, a counselor, a teacher, and a school administrator.

**3. Does this mean he or she is retarded?**

No. Probably your child's intelligence is in the average range or higher. The problem is that your child may not be able to function in a regular classroom without special help. The testing will pinpoint the kind of help your child needs.

**4. Will she be in a special class?**

No, probably not. Special education changed with the passage of the Individuals with Disabilities Education Act (IDEA). This landmark legislation moved children with special needs from segregated classrooms into regular classrooms.

**5. What if I decide that special education isn't a good idea for my child?**

That's your decision, and it's up to the school district to work out an alternate program that meets your child's needs.

**6. What are my options?**

You have several options if you decide not to place him in special education: One, you may keep your child in the regular classroom. He won't be labeled, but he may not receive the

## Two Mothers' Stories

I believe that inclusion in regular education will work with severely disabled children. My son is a Down syndrome child. He's sixteen and in the ninth grade. He speaks in one- to four-word sentences. When he was ten he was placed in a neighborhood school instead of riding a bus across town to his special education class. He doesn't see himself as different. He has been included in birthday parties with non-disabled peers and attends school dances. He has wonderful behavior and social skills. He has been able to go everywhere and do everything we can get him involved in.

Dora

Both of my daughters receive special education services. My thirteen-year-old daughter is blind. She is fully included in school and has a part-time aide. Her fifteen-year-old sister is autistic; although she has benefited from inclusion, more attention to social skills and building on her individual strengths would have been a plus. I was fortunate enough to have a principal with whom I could actually discuss things. We didn't always agree, but I feel we had enough respect for each other to compromise when we had differing views.

Pat

help he needs. Two, you could enroll your child in a private school. Although no label will be attached to him, the services available may not be as complete as in a public school. Three, you may choose to homeschool your child. He or she will receive individual attention, but switching between the role of parent and teacher is difficult and exhausting.

## The Benefits of Inclusion

When the 1975 Individuals with Disabilities Education Act (IDEA) became law, special education changed. This landmark legislation mandated that children with special needs be included in the regular classroom. A few of the benefits of inclusion are listed below.

### 9 Facts about Inclusion

1. Students with disabilities are included in the regular school program. Special education services are provided in the classroom rather than in a special room or school.
2. Instruction is provided in the least restrictive environment (LRE). Many special needs students are capable of receiving education in a regular classroom.
3. Academic requirements may differ. Special needs children's academic requirements and social standards may not be the same as other students. For example, a child who has problems writing might give an oral report rather than a written one.
4. The Individualized Education Program (IEP) guides the education of special needs children. The IEP is designed to create a sound educational environment for the child.
5. Children without disabilities benefit from inclusion. Children in classrooms that include disabled kids show a greater acceptance of children who are different from themselves.
6. Inclusion improves learning. Students without disabilities often do better academically because a teacher is more apt to break down instruction into its essential parts.
7. Children learn to accept individual differences. The best way to help children overcome misconceptions about kids who have disabilities is to bring them together in an integrated setting.
8. Children develop new friendships. Children with disabilities who are included in a regular classroom develop friendships

in their home communities, while special education students sent to regional special education programs may become oddballs in their communities.

9. Parent participation is increased. When children with disabilities are integrated into regular schools, parents have more opportunity to participate in their school and in the community where their school is located.

## A Picture of Successful Inclusion

1. Students receive instructional supports that maximize their participation in the general education curriculum and their engagement in the general population.
2. Teachers use a variety of strategies, including curriculum and instructional adaptations, peer tutoring, cooperative learning, and modified curriculum.

## A Collaborative Inclusion Project

The Circle of Inclusion Project consists of three collaborative projects between the University of Kansas and local school districts. All three projects implement programs of inclusive early childhood special instruction. Here's how inclusion works at White Elementary School in Wichita, Kansas, a school that serves about three hundred four- to seven-year-old children:

1. Children are placed in two half-day pre-kindergarten classes and six first-grade classes.
2. Children enrolled in special education attend regular education classrooms with their peers.
3. Each inclusive classroom consists of approximately fifteen regular education students and four or five students enrolled in special education.
4. Special needs children see other children with skills they can model.

135

5. Regular education students learn that everyone has strengths of some kind and everyone has challenges.

6. Children learn at an early age to be patient and tolerant and that all children should be treated fairly, with care and compassion.[4]

## Champions of Inclusion

Inclusion champions are those who adapt and utilize strategies and materials to help students with disabilities learn and succeed. Here are some examples from Bill Henderson, principal of Patrick O'Hearn Elementary School in Boston:

1. The classmates who figure out ways for an autistic child to participate in the group's skit depicting a scene from the American Revolutionary War.
2. The special education teacher who writes a simplified version of *Romeo and Juliet* for Juan so that he can grasp the key points of the play being discussed in his eleventh-grade literature class.
3. A behavior consultant who crafts a positive behavior plan for Rakeem so that he can stay on task more and become more successful.
4. The speech therapist who organizes a set of picture symbols and voice recordings for Betsy so that she can communicate her needs more effectively.
5. The fifth-grade teacher who learns how to use a computer with screen reading software so that Timothy can follow some of the popular books read by his classmates.
6. The basketball coach who designates and arranges tasks for a Down syndrome child so that she can serve as the assistant manager for her friend's team.
7. The occupational therapist who coordinates a school store where students with fine motor and social needs can practice useful tasks.

8. The biology teacher who makes a chart for Joshua to help him take responsibility for some of the activities in the lab.
9. The teacher's aide who uses unobtrusive signals to keep a child on task.
10. The art teacher who keeps a box of different-sized grips with her so that students with fine motor difficulties can manipulate drawing and painting equipment.
11. The child who shows his class a more efficient way to solve a math problem.[5]

# 10

## How Good Families
## Make Good Schools

Research shows that students with parents who are involved in their child's education are more successful in school regardless of race or income level. In fact, experts say that the key to school success is parents' involvement in their children's education. If a child knows that his parents and teachers are working together, the child is more likely to see his education as a high priority, and he will make a commitment to it.

### You Can Make a Difference

Parental involvement in your child's education can have different meanings. It might begin with the simple question, "How did you do in school today?" In the following sections we'll look at some ways you can make a difference by staying involved.

### 7 Ways to Get Involved in Your Child's Education

1. Read to your child every day.
2. Check your child's homework, keep track of assignments, and give assistance when your child doesn't understand an assignment.
3. Don't wait for scheduled parent-teacher conferences; instead regularly take a few minutes to discuss your children's progress with their teachers. (*"Hi, how is Sylvia doing today?"*)
4. Vote in school board elections and support good legislation for public schools.
5. Support high academic standards for all grade levels.
6. Set standards for TV watching on school nights. Limit TV viewing and stress the fact that homework comes first.
7. Support efforts to provide better education in your school and state.

### 9 Good Results of Parent Involvement

Over and over, major educational research studies have shown how important it is for parents to be involved in their children's schools. Here are some of the findings of these major studies.

1. When parents are involved in their child's education at home, the child does better in school.
2. The children of parents who participate in school go farther in school and attend better schools.
3. The involved family makes critical contributions to the child's achievement from preschool through high school.
4. Encouraging education is more important to achievement than income, educational level, or cultural background.
5. Reading aloud to children is the most important activity leading to an increased chance of reading success. Talking about books and reading to children from books improves reading achievement.

6. Regular talk at home about school equals better academic performance and higher achievement.
7. Kids' achievement is higher when parents organize home study time, monitor that time, help with homework, and discuss school.
8. The earlier parent involvement begins at home, the better the effects.
9. Other positive results include improved achievement in all subjects, reduced absenteeism, better behavior, and greater parent confidence in the child.

## 8 Facts about Parent Involvement

1. Families provide the primary educational environment.
2. The most accurate predictor of school success is a home setting that encourages learning.
3. Parents who participate in their child's education improve the student's achievement.
4. Comprehensive, long lasting, and well-planned parent participation is the most effective.
5. Positive benefits of parent involvement extend through high school.
6. Children from culturally and racially diverse or low-income families have the most to gain from parent input.
7. The extent of parent involvement is more important to school success than family income or education.
8. Students with parents who take an active role in their education are more likely to attend school regularly, earn higher grades, pass their classes, and graduate.[1]

## 10 Ways to Prevent Home and School Problems

1. Talk with your child's teacher about what your child will learn and be expected to do during the school year.
2. Find out how you can help your child at home with school-related projects.

3. Make learning a priority in your home by providing a time and place for children to study.
4. Visit your child's classroom to learn more about the instructor's teaching style.
5. Ask your child's teacher for updates on his progress and where he might need help.
6. Take advantage of the library, after-school tutoring, field trips, and summer camps that encourage learning.
7. Get involved in community, school, and volunteer activities.
8. Together look into different colleges or read about interesting careers.
9. Visit a college campus or a job site with your child.
10. Turn off the television during meals and talk with your child about current events, books, or movies.

## What Makes a Good School?

Good schools share some common characteristics. Here are eight signs of a quality school:

1. *High expectations for every student.* Expectations that recognize all students can learn and reach their full potential if provided with the correct tools and services.
2. *Parent and community support.* Parents who actively support their community schools and work to strengthen student learning.
3. *A rigorous curriculum and fair assessment.* A school curriculum that develops student knowledge and critical thinking, and testing that accurately measures the achievement of students.
4. *Sufficient resources to help students achieve.* Schools that provide the necessary resources for all students to achieve.
5. *Safe, healthy, and supportive learning environment.* Schools where students can learn and grow.

6. *Schools and classrooms equipped for teaching and learning.* Schools with up-to-date textbooks, resources, and technology to aid student study and research.
7. *Qualified teachers in every classroom.* Teachers with the appropriate degrees, teaching certificates, and skills for the subjects they teach.
8. *Strong school leadership.* Fully qualified school principals who make informed decisions that promote learning.[2]

## Saving Failing Schools

Big changes can happen when communities are determined to change struggling schools. Here are four examples of how parents played a part in reversing the decline of their schools or school districts.

### Example 1: Chattanooga, Tennessee

In 2000, Chattanooga was home to nine of the worst elementary schools in the state. Only 18 percent of third graders were reading at or above grade level. But in 2006, 74 percent of the kids tested as proficient or advanced in reading. The once-failing schools scored better than 90 percent of all the schools in the state. Here's what happened:

1. Chattanooga's Public Education Foundation (PEF) recommended a quality teacher in every room.
2. Teachers had to reapply for their jobs.
3. One hundred teachers left the district.
4. Teachers and principals went through required retraining.
5. The local university offered a free master's degree program for teachers in the failing schools.
6. Community volunteers joined with parents to help them read to their children at home.

7. The Urban League started an after-school literacy program for kids.[3]

## Example 2: Long Beach, California

Long Beach has the country's third highest youth poverty rate, and only a few of the children at the Stevenson YMCA Community School can afford to buy lunch. Still, the school was named a California Distinguished School. The partnership between the YMCA and the school was a winner.

The YMCA, with the help of the teachers, operates inside the school by running the after-school program. Here are the results since the beginning of the partnership:

1. Parent attitudes about school and education have improved.
2. About two hundred parents and community residents are involved in the program.
3. An after-school program encourages a love of reading.
4. The program trains parents in literacy skills, and then those parents go out and teach other parents.
5. The school offers parents computer and English classes.
6. Parents collected about seven hundred signatures to get repairs made to broken cement sidewalks near the school.[4]

## Example 3: Cleveland Heights, Ohio

The Cleveland high school was two-tiered, with only the self-motivated students going to the best colleges. But that changed when the school joined Ohio's High School Transformation Initiative to turn large schools into small communities. Cleveland Heights High School was transformed into five small schools within the building with the following results:

1. Forums were started where parents and community members shared their hopes for the school with teachers and administrators.

144

2. Boards including students, parents, teachers, and community leaders were formed to guide the school's direction.
3. Five principals walked the halls and called the students by their names.
4. The school is now rated effective on the annual Ohio Report Card.[5]

### Example 4: Sacramento, California

While some considered the Susan B. Anthony School a throwaway school or a school in peril, new principal Carol Sharp believed that it was a school that had lost touch with the community, reports Roberta Furger for the George Lucas Educational Foundation. She writes, "That was in 1998. Today, the kindergarten-through-sixth-grade school has been transformed. Student achievement has skyrocketed, suspensions have been all but eliminated, and parents are respected partners, not outsiders." Here's how it happened:

1. A plan to involve parents was developed.
2. Teachers and staff began to visit the homes of students to share information about the school.
3. At first the parents felt they didn't belong in the school, and many expressed anger and frustration because they felt shut out by the school.
4. Parents were reluctant to participate in the school, but when they were asked to come to school, they did.
5. The teachers and staff worked with the parents to identify their needs and concerns.
6. A successful partnership between parents and teachers resulted.[6]

## Breaking Down Barriers

Do you feel disconnected from your child's teacher or school? Perhaps the teacher didn't answer your questions at the last conference or for some other reason you feel isolated from the school. Instead of expressing your anger, communicate your feelings through "I" messages as opposed to "You" messages. "I" messages explain how you feel about behavior. "You" messages berate, accuse, and tear down an individual's self-esteem.

The following quiz is based on some real-life scenarios. Read each one and choose the answer that best describes the parent who can express feelings without berating or accusing the teacher.

1. Your ten-year-old didn't deserve the low score she received on an English test. You should approach her teacher with:
   (a) "I think you gave Sally the wrong grade in English."
   (b) "What in the world did she do to deserve that kind of a grade?"
   (c) "I don't get it. Explain this grade for me."
   (d) "Could we talk a few minutes about Sally's grade?"
2. Your seventh-grade son lost his lunch money two days in a row, and you're determined to find out what happened to the money. The right approach is to:
   (a) accuse the teacher of mishandling the lunch money
   (b) discuss with the teacher ways to help him keep track of his money
   (c) do nothing since the responsibility is his; no money, no lunch
3. The teacher informs you that your child has a reading disability and needs some special education help. You say:
   (a) "I think you're wrong! He reads to me every night after supper."
   (b) "I can't understand it; I was always a good reader."
   (c) "Explain the program to me."
4. Jason's teacher kept him after school to finish an overdue homework assignment. You're angry with the teacher be-

cause your child missed Little League practice. You should say:

(a) "You should have contacted me; he missed an important practice."

(b) "In the future, if he's going to stay after school, would you please notify me as early as possible?"

(c) "I want a day's notice before you keep my child after school."

5. You are upset because your child brings home so much schoolwork she can hardly carry it all in her backpack. You make an appointment with the teacher and say:

(a) "What's all this homework about? I think it's criminal."

(b) "I think my daughter's back is bent permanently from carrying her books."

(c) "What can we do to lighten the workload she brings home?"

6. The teacher has requested psychological testing for your child. You say:

(a) "I told Delbert you want him tested, and now he's worried sick."

(b) "I don't like the idea of tests for my kid."

(c) "Please understand, I don't like tests, and Delbert is scared."

7. Your daughter is having trouble keeping up with the class in reading, and the teacher has requested a conference to talk about the problem. You say:

(a) "I told you at the beginning of school that she can't read and needs help."

(b) "I'm glad we can talk about this. It's been a problem for a long time."

**Check your answers:** You got your point across without accusing or berating the teacher if you chose the following answers: 1. (d), 2. (b), 3. (c), 4. (b), 5. (c), 6. (c), 7. (b).

## General Rules for Parent-Teacher Conferences

### At the Conference

1. Avoid angry or apologetic reactions. Instead, ask for examples.
2. Ask what is being done about the problem and what strategies seem to help at school.
3. Develop an action plan that includes steps for parents to take at home and steps the teacher will take if the problem comes up at school.
4. Schedule a follow-up conference and decide on the best way to stay in touch (phone, email, or letters sent to the home).
5. Discuss your child's habits, hobbies, concerns, and other topics that may help the teacher understand and work with her.

### After the Conference

1. Be positive about the conference as you discuss it with your child.
2. Talk over the decisions made, and include both the good and the problems, if any.
3. If an action plan was developed, explain when it will start.
4. With the action plan in place, stay in touch with the teacher, and regularly monitor your child's behavior, class work, and homework.
5. Thank the teacher for his help in your child's school success.[7]

## Strategies for Handling Conflicts and Disagreements

1. Parents and school staff members must work closely together to address the issues.
2. It is essential for both parties to realize that the goals for the child are shared goals.
3. Both must agree that the child's interest comes first.

4. Avoid confrontation, deal specifically with solutions to the identified issues, and be prepared to offer alternatives.
5. Always deal with the issues, not the emotions of the people involved. Decide where you can compromise; effective resolution usually requires some form of compromise.
6. Be sure that your expectations are realistic and reasonable. Specify both long-term and short-term goals and state when a follow-up visit should occur.
7. Both parties need to commit to the recommended solutions and agree jointly.[8]

# 11

# Success through Homeschooling

Over a million children are being taught at home, according to data in a study conducted in the 2001–2002 school year by the National Home Education Research Institute (NHERI) in Salem, Oregon. But compared to the total number of children being educated in U.S. public schools, the figure is relatively small. Still, parents continue to believe in the benefits of homeschooling: children can work at their own pace, they aren't bored with their studies, and there are fewer discipline problems than in public school.

## All about Homeschooling

Parents choose to homeschool their children for a variety of reasons, and they educate them in a variety of ways. Let's look at some of the facts about homeschooling today.

### Quiz: Homeschooling Fact or Fiction

Not everything you hear about homeschooling is true. The following true-false test is designed to set straight some misconceptions about homeschooling. Be sure to check the answers at the end of the quiz.

|  | True | False |
|---|---|---|
| 1. Children perform better at home than in a classroom. | ____ | ____ |
| 2. Online learning aids homeschoolers. | ____ | ____ |
| 3. A good reason for homeschooling is moral instruction. | ____ | ____ |
| 4. The environment of public schools is a minor concern of parents. | ____ | ____ |
| 5. Homeschoolers score higher on achievement tests. | ____ | ____ |
| 6. Admission to college is a problem for homeschool kids. | ____ | ____ |
| 7. Homeschoolers don't get along with their peers. | ____ | ____ |
| 8. Homeschool children are socially active. | ____ | ____ |
| 9. Online courses for kids are too easy. | ____ | ____ |
| 10. Gifted and talented kids prefer a traditional classroom. | ____ | ____ |
| 11. Low achievement test scores are a result of homeschooling. | ____ | ____ |
| 12. Homeschooled children never get involved in clubs or groups. | ____ | ____ |
| 13. Homeschooling strengthens family ties and family values. | ____ | ____ |
| 14. Homeschooling is illegal in most states. | ____ | ____ |
| 15. U.S. law requires a teaching certificate to teach at home. | ____ | ____ |
| 16. Homeschooled children usually take a few courses online. | ____ | ____ |
| 17. Curriculum packages are hard to find. | ____ | ____ |
| 18. There is very little regulation of homeschools at the state level. | ____ | ____ |
| 19. Public support for high school homeschool programs is poor. | ____ | ____ |
| 20. Online learning is only for gifted and talented children. | ____ | ____ |

**Answers:** 1. True; 2. True; 3. True; 4. False; 5. True; 6. False; 7. False; 8. True; 9. False; 10. False; 11. False; 12. False; 13. True; 14. False; 15. False; 16. True; 17. False; 18. True; 19. True; 20. False.

## The Legal Status of Homeschooling

1. Homeschooling is legal in all states.
2. State law generally requires parents to file basic information with the state or the school district.
3. Over half of states require some form of testing to evaluate the child's academic progress.
4. Some states may accept a portfolio evaluation or a teacher evaluation.
5. A few states have education or testing requirements for parents.
6. Some states require submission of a curriculum plan.
7. Parents do not need teaching certificates.
8. Some state statutes mandate that local districts provide access to curricular and extracurricular programs for home-school students who wish to use them.[1]

## 6 Reasons Parents Homeschool Their Children

In 2003 the National Center for Education Statistics conducted a nationwide survey of homeschooling parents of children five to seventeen years old. The parents were asked a series of questions about their reasons for homeschooling their children. Here is what they said their reasons were. (Note that since the parents were allowed to choose more than one reason on the survey, the percentages do not add up to 100 percent.)

1. Concern about the environment of other schools (85%)
2. To provide religious or moral instruction (72%)
3. Dissatisfaction with the academic instruction of other schools (68%)
4. Child has other special needs (29%)
5. Child has medical or mental health problems (16%)
6. Other reasons (20%)

## 9 Advantages of Homeschooling

1. Parents are with their child all day.
2. Homeschooled children avoid inappropriate peer pressure.
3. Parents and other adults are the primary role models.
4. Children learn to interact with people of all ages.
5. Home education promotes good communication and emotional closeness between family members.
6. Homeschooling develops a positive home influence and parental involvement.
7. Education may be tailored to the child's learning style, interests, and learning pace.
8. The child is allowed to mature at his or her own speed.
9. Family values are strengthened.

## 10 Disadvantages of Homeschooling

1. Researchers can't say homeschooled children do better or worse academically than traditional school children, because they are unable to get a representative sample of homeschoolers.
2. There is no way to tell if children who test above average at home would or wouldn't do the same or better in a public school setting.
3. It is difficult to determine the adjustment of homeschool children because they spend less time with same-age peers.
4. Parents must be prepared to spend all day with their children.
5. Parents must supervise lessons, check progress, think of activities, and make worksheets.
6. Parents who decide to homeschool will go against the norm and must expect to be grilled by other parents.
7. Twenty-four hours a day with children plus being their teacher is no joke.

8. Materials are expensive, so home education isn't cheaper than public school education.
9. A parent may need to quit his or her job to be a full-time homeschool teacher.
10. Even if you are not in the mood, you have to appear enthusiastic about the material you are teaching.

## 9 Facts about Homeschools

1. By the beginning of the twentieth century, public schools were becoming commonplace.
2. After compulsory education laws were put in place, only a few states allowed home instruction.
3. Today homeschooling is legal in all states.
4. In 2003 the National Center for Education Statistics reported that about 1,996,000 students in grades K to 12 are in full- or part-time homeschools.
5. Homeschooling families tend to be middle class and have more children.
6. Parents who homeschool are more likely to vote, give money to political causes, and contact elected officials.
7. Families that choose to educate their children at home come from all major ethnic, cultural, and religious backgrounds.
8. Over half of all states require some kind of testing evaluation. Other states may accept a portfolio evaluation or teacher's evaluation.
9. Parents do not need teaching certificates.[2]

## Making Homeschool Work

There may be as many ways to do home education as there are families doing it. Today's homeschooling parents have more options than ever to help them create a quality educational experience.

## Online and Distance Learning

Homeschool parents use a variety of materials and methods for instruction, including distance learning. Distance learning courses provide instruction using some type of technology to communicate between the student and instructor. Here are some facts about distance learning:

1. Almost one-half of students who were homeschooled in 2003 engaged in some sort of distance learning.
2. Approximately 20 percent of homeschooled students took a course or received instruction provided by television, video, or radio.
3. Homeschooled students may take a course or receive instruction provided over the Internet, email, or the World Wide Web.
4. Homeschooled students may take a correspondence course by mail designed specifically for children who learn at home.
5. Parents of homeschooled students use a variety of sources for curricula and books.[3]

## 10 Facts about Online or Virtual Schools

A U.S. Department of Education survey found that high school students saw the advantages of online learning. The survey established that 36 percent of the nation's school districts had students enrolled in virtual schools, mostly in high schools.[4] Here are some points to consider about online classes:

1. Online courses fit the schedules of kids who devote large blocks of time to such activities as ballet, acting, or tennis.
2. Online learning frees students who dislike the traditional school atmosphere and the pressure to conform.
3. Students who need to work can arrange their schedules around their job requirements.

4. Virtual schools benefit students who want a customized education rather than the old-style daily schedule of classes.
5. Online courses are one way students can make up a failed course.
6. Online courses are a way to add courses that students cannot fit into their regular school schedule.
7. Online courses allow students to take advanced placement tests.
8. Virtual education excludes hands-on laboratory classes such as chemistry and biology.
9. Some educators fear students will cheat and use the work of someone else.
10. A virtual education may result in a loss of social interaction.

## 8 Resources for Homeschool Families

Parents are the primary resource for homeschooled children. Usually mothers take the lead and fathers pitch in when they can. Estimates suggest that one in ten fathers takes primary responsibility for their child's instruction. Resources for homeschooling parents include:

1. Local and state support groups that offer advice and assistance
2. Families that sometimes share the instructional duties
3. At least one state-level organization in every state
4. Book fairs or association meetings where parents can inspect materials
5. Libraries, museums, colleges, and parks departments
6. Publishers' curricular packages, books, and periodical materials available for inspection and purchase
7. Enrollment in independent study programs or enrollment as a part-time student, which some states offer homeschooled children

## Distance Learning

After Ben Hathaway's father was called to active duty in the Army National Guard, the fifteen-year-old had to help his family tend the 130 head of cattle on their 345-acre farm in Tennessee. Traditional school ate up too many daylight hours. Here's how he solved his problem:

Ben started taking courses from a Lutheran high school 1,750 miles away in California. He studied algebra and world history on his own. Because he didn't have to sit for six hours a day, he could play a little on the computer and come back later. Ben misses high school social events like dances, but he doesn't miss the pressure to perform and be like everyone else.[5]

8. Instructional support through homeschool resource centers and part-time enrollment of homeschool children offered by some public schools

### Homeschool Co-ops

Choosing the best homeschool program for your child takes time and research. Some parents prefer a strict classroom style with playtime outdoors, while others choose a prepackaged curriculum. Others combine their skills to form a homeschool co-op. A co-op means classroom instruction is given by different parents according to who is skilled in a specific subject.

1. Parents in a co-op are like-minded in their goals.
2. Children learn in a traditional classroom setting, but their parents are the teachers.

3. Parents share the teaching load. For instance, a parent who loves science becomes the science teacher, and the parent with writing skills teaches creative writing.
4. A co-op can supplement a family's education plan.
5. A co-op takes care of the overflow of subjects that parents have a difficult time fitting into their teaching schedules.
6. A co-op helps new homeschool families start an instructional program by giving them ideas for lessons and lesson plans.

## Socialization

Many educators feel that homeschooling limits a child's social contacts and ability to get along with others. But homeschooling doesn't mean a child is desk-bound for six or seven hours and then spends the evening studying for the next day's subjects. For concerned parents, Isabelle Shaw, a homeschooling mom, suggests the following ways to develop a child's socialization skills.

### 5 Ways to Develop Socialization

Socialization takes place every day. It depends on how the child sees you, the parent, interact with others and how you interact with your own child. Here's how to develop your child's social skills.

1. Make friends with other homeschooling families. To get acquainted, check the Internet, your church, and the library in your community.
2. Encourage your child to join a youth group or children's club—for example church, crafts, 4-H, Boy Scouts or Girl Scouts, or environmental groups.
3. When you meet families during school hours, ask if they homeschool. If they say yes, you have the start of a new friendship.

4. Find out about sports programs available through the recreation department.
5. Visit nursing homes, senior centers, shelters, etc., and volunteer to help the residents. Let your child see how you unselfishly give yourself to your community.[6]

## Choosing a Curriculum

Parents who decide to homeschool their children may be overwhelmed by the number and claims of curriculum publishers. The following review of homeschool curriculum publishers will help you decide on the best program for your child.

### Calvert School

Calvert School has been serving homeschooling families for over one hundred years. Its time-tested lessons are designed to appeal to different learning styles. The Calvert website says, "Our program is proven and assures you no gaps in instruction. In addition to our lessons we support your home instruction with our Placement Testing, Education Counselors, and Advisory Teaching Services."[7] Calvert School provides the following services:

1. A preschool through third-grade placement program that helps parents choose the correct grade level and provides assessment tools for a self-test for grade level readiness.
2. A required free placement test to be administered by the parent of fourth- through eighth-grade children.
3. An optional Advisory Teaching Service. Eight times a year the Advisory Teacher evaluates tests in each subject area.
4. The Advisory Teacher stays in contact with the parent and teacher and offers instructional support.
5. Several versions of the curriculum are offered to fit the child's ability.

6. Some of the child's lessons may be modified to take advantage of a preferred learning style.

## K12, Inc.

K12 is a leading online school curriculum provider serving thousands of students in kindergarten through high school. Developed by education experts, K12 curriculum is based on time-tested and research-based methods of instruction. It provides flexible, individualized learning approaches and courses that combine online interactive lessons, printed materials, and offline activities.

According to the K12 website, "K12 brings learning and possibility alive in all kinds of minds—fast minds, wandering minds, those that need a little more time, and those that just get lost in the shuffle of a traditional classroom. Passionate, professional teachers are connected virtually to help kids find the pace and learning style that works best for them."[8] Courses for students in kindergarten through ninth grade provide:

1. Over 700 lessons per grade.
2. Six subjects: language arts/English, math, science, history, art, and music.
3. Planning and progress tools for parents.
4. Lessons based on Core Knowledge sequence.
5. Online worksheets, lesson plans, and teaching guides.
6. Traditional materials such as books, CDs, science equipment, manipulatives, art supplies, etc.
7. Courses that meet or exceed every state's academic standards.[9]

## Laurel Springs School

Laurel Springs School is a kindergarten through twelfth grade accredited distance learning school located in Ojai, California. It provides homeschool education that uses each child's learning style. The school's mission is based on the belief that each child is distinctive and has unique interests, talents, and learning styles. Laurel Springs School offers the following:

1. A curriculum that develops creative and critical thinking.
2. A curriculum that can be mixed and matched to fit the child's needs.
3. Project-based curriculum for kindergarten through eighth grades that integrates language arts, math, social studies, science, the arts, and health.
4. Hands-on projects based on classic literature.
5. Project-based curriculum for high school students that encourages a variety of learning assignments.
6. Learning projects that encourage the use of the students' own learning styles.[10]

## A Beka Academy Traditional Homeschool Program

One of the programs A Beka Academy offers is a traditional homeschool program. Their website states, "The A Beka Academy Traditional Parent-Directed program has courses available for five-year-old kindergarten and grades one through twelve. This parent-directed program provides you with all the necessary A Beka Book student and teacher materials needed to complete an entire grade."[11] Some highlights of the program are:

1. You can teach without teacher training or experience.
2. Easy-to-follow, step-by-step instructions make this possible.
3. The Traditional Program has courses available for kindergarten through grade 12.
4. This program provides parents with all the necessary student and teacher materials needed to complete an entire grade or course.

5. Included are textbooks, workbooks, class and homework assignments, and tests.

## A Beka Academy DVD Program

A Beka Academy also offers a DVD-based program. Their website says, "DVD courses with master teachers are available in Program 1 for five-year-old kindergarten and grades one through twelve. Under the parent's supervision, students in grades nine through twelve receive credit toward graduation requirements and can earn a diploma from A Beka Academy. On a scheduled periodic basis, work is sent to the A Beka Academy Office for evaluation." For this program, A Beka provides:

1. All necessary textbooks, tests, keys, and DVDs to complete grade/courses selected.
2. Manual with daily lesson plans.
3. Grade-level placement based upon review of previous work completed.
4. An academic calendar.
5. Progress reports for record keeping.
6. Return mailing envelopes for student work and prepaid return labels for DVDs (for contiguous U.S. and Canada).
7. Evaluation of student work for each grading period.
8. A report card after each grading period.
9. Credit toward graduation once all lessons have been viewed, assignments and tests have been completed, and passing grades have been earned.
10. A plan of study to meet graduation requirements for college preparatory program of study.
11. A diploma acknowledging completion of graduation requirements.
12. An annual graduation ceremony.
13. One copy of the transcript free of charge.[12]

## Sonlight Curriculum

Sonlight Curriculum offers several literature-based Core Programs. Their website says, "Curriculum books are chosen not merely for their academic value, but for their value as important additions to your personal family library. These are books that will not just educate, but will entertain and inspire."[13]

1. *CoreUltra Packages* include everything parents need to teach one student for an entire year. The packages include a Core Program plus language arts, handwriting, math, science, and electives (art, music), plus the required resources needed.
2. *CorePlus Packages* include a core program of language arts, science, and electives; they do not include math, handwriting, or required resources. They provide the flexibility to match the child's skill levels in math and handwriting.
3. *Core Packages* include the "cores" of the curriculum: history, Bible, reading, and memorization/public speaking. Parents may tailor their child's education by choosing the math, language arts, and electives they prefer for their child.

Sonlight Curriculum says, "Because our Core programs are literature based and our Science programs center on discovery-oriented books and experiments, you'll find that a broad age-range of students will enjoy learning the same material, and you yourself will enjoy what you're reading. The books aren't dumbed down. They present the fundamental information every student needs, but they also convey unexpected tidbits that will engage you as well."

# 12

# Don't Forget about Values

Rules are a must for a smooth-running family, but parents can get bogged down in rules at the expense of values. Research suggests that less learning goes on in families with an abundance of rules than in families where right and wrong values are stressed.

Children develop virtues when their parents present a clear set of values about right and wrong, display those values by their own example, and encourage their children to decide which behavior exemplifies those values. In the long run it's the values children learn from their parents, not the number of rules, that help them succeed in school. The choices your child makes at school are based on the values he learns from you.

## When Children Challenge Rules and Values

The following quiz is based on some real-life scenarios. Read each one and choose the best response.

1. Alice is glued to the TV. In spite of your rule forbidding TV before her homework is finished, she isn't moving. What do you do?
   (a) Turn off the TV and escort her to her workplace.
   (b) Do nothing. Homework is her problem.
   (c) Threaten to restrict her for two weeks.

The best answer is (a). Threats don't work. But if you do nothing, Alice may continue to ignore you. Turn off the TV and check to see that she has her books and materials. The rest is up to Alice.

2. Your son, Jack, is suspended from middle school. The counselor said Jack dipped a classmate's hat in the toilet, poured water on the boy's head, and punched him out. You should:
   (a) ignore the incident.
   (b) talk to Jack and get his side of the story.
   (c) call a school board member and complain about the poor teaching, counseling, and discipline at the school.

The correct answer is (b). Talk to Jack and get his side of the story. Don't make accusations until both sides are heard.

3. Thirteen-year-old Jennifer doesn't like to shower. Each day she exits the bathroom combing her damp hair and leaving her clothes and a soggy towel in a pile. Suspicious, you check on her and find her reading a novel while the empty shower sprays hot water. Your reaction is to:
   (a) blow up when she says, "I use deodorant. I don't need to shower every day."
   (b) say, "The importance of a daily shower has been established as one of our family rules."
   (c) talk to her about trust and truthfulness.

166

Was your answer (b)? This is a clear case of breaking a family rule. Also talk to Jennifer about trust and truthfulness, two important values.

4. Josh and his friend are playing a game on the family computer. You overhear them talking about making and selling copies of the game. Josh knows what they are planning is dishonest. You should:
(a) ignore the conversation. It's Josh's decision.
(b) say, "You can't do that. It's dishonest."
(c) lecture the kids on copyright law.

The correct answer is (b). Josh knows that pirating software is dishonest. Since honesty is an important value, you can't ignore what they are planning.

## Make Smart Family Rules

Newspaper columnist Kathleen Brown tells of a fifteen-year-old's creative interpretation of her parents' "no cigarettes and no smoking in the house" rule: The girl would invite the neighbor boy to meet her in the backyard under her bedroom window. He would light up, and while she hung out the window, he would offer her drags from his cigarette. When her mother asked about the pile of cigarette butts under her window, she claimed they didn't belong to her. She swore that she had no cigarettes in the house and she wasn't smoking.

According to Brown, the loopholes could have been plugged if the teen's mom had said the following:

1. "You will not have any cigarettes in your possession."
2. "You will not bring cigarettes in the house."
3. "You will not smoke inside or outside the house."[1]

## Rules That Reflect Values

Smart family rules reflect and come out of family values.

| Family Values | Family Rules | How Rules Reflect Child's Values |
|---|---|---|
| Education | Finish homework before watching TV | Places value on education |
| Love | Watch out and care for each other | Shows kindness toward others |
| Hard work | Do your best | Doesn't avoid difficult tasks |
| Honesty | Always tell the truth | Learns to tell the truth even when lying is easier |
| Morality | Do what you know is right | Follows his or her conscience |
| Religious faith | Accept different views | Tolerates other's faith |
| Respect for others | No ethnic jokes or comments that demean someone else | Accepts people of other races |
| Responsibility | If you say you will do something, do it | Takes responsibility for actions |
| See both sides of an argument | Listen to opinions you don't agree with | Makes a decision after considering all the facts |
| Thoughtfulness | Be considerate of others | Anticipates wants and needs of others |

## Values and Rules That Work Together

The following exercise will give you a chance to compare your use of values with the number and kind of rules used in your family. Parents can easily get bogged down in rules, but rules are a must for a smooth-running family.

1. Divide a sheet of notebook paper into two columns.
2. In the first column, list the spiritual and moral values important to your family. Do you want your child to develop self-control? To tell the truth? To value hard work?

3. In the second column, jot down the family rules. Do you want your child to come home on time? To complete homework without an argument? To go to bed on time?
4. Study your list of rules and eliminate useless ones.
5. Evaluate your list for any values you may have overlooked that you want to build in your family.
6. Finally, ask yourself the question, "Am I doing my best to live up to the standards that I teach my children?"

| Our family's values | Our family's rules |
|---|---|
| 1. _____ | 1. _____ |
| 2. _____ | 2. _____ |
| 3. _____ | 3. _____ |
| 4. _____ | 4. _____ |
| 5. _____ | 5. _____ |

| Values we want to develop | Rules we can eliminate |
|---|---|
| 1. _____ | 1. _____ |
| 2. _____ | 2. _____ |
| 3. _____ | 3. _____ |
| 4. _____ | 4. _____ |
| 5. _____ | 5. _____ |

Do I model the values I want my child to learn? How can I improve?

1. _____

2. _____

3. _____

4. _____

5. _____

## Passing On Your Values

To help you evaluate your values, check out the following ways to teach important virtues to children.

### 7 Ways to Teach Patience

Can children learn patience in today's fast-paced world? Marilyn Benoit, a child and adolescent psychiatrist and president of the American Academy of Child and Adolescent Psychiatry, told the story of her grandniece, a technologically savvy toddler. On a shopping trip the child lost control when a store clerk wouldn't let her play with a display computer. "He won't let me do www.com!" the two-year-old complained loudly before dissolving into a fit of tears.

Benoit describes the meltdown in "The Dot.com Kids and the Demise of Frustration Tolerance," an essay she wrote for the Alliance for Childhood. Like other experts, she sees such outbursts as part of a disturbing trend. According to Benoit, many parents overload their children with activities and computer games that may add to the frantic pace of life and limit children's ability to learn patience.[2]

Learning to wait and to take turns are important elements of learning patience. Try these seven patience-building strategies:

1. *Model patience.* When you have to wait, your words and body language signal how you feel, and your child learns from your behavior. Instead of complaining when you're stuck in traffic, turn on some relaxing music.
2. *Help your child verbalize her emotions.* Young children don't have the vocabulary to express how they feel. If it's a long wait in the grocery store checkout line say, "I know you're tired, but you're doing a great job waiting."
3. *Don't expect too much.* If you're eating out, ask your server for a small bowl of fruit for a snack until your child's meal is served.

170

Dorothy Law Nolte, author of *Children Learn What They Live: Parenting to Inspire Values*, recommends that parents engage children in slow-paced, enriching activities. Watch a sunset with your child and talk about the subtle changes in the color of the sky as the sun drops below the horizon.

4. *Bring crayons and a coloring book.* When you must wait, help your child by providing crayons and a coloring book or a storybook you can read together.
5. *Keep a watch or timer handy.* If you need to finish what you're doing, set an egg timer for five minutes and say, "When the bell rings, I'll read a book to you."
6. For older kids (preschool, primary, and upper grades), *don't reward impatience.* Children must learn that they can't always get what they want. And they will show their impatience by throwing temper tantrums, being mean to a sibling, or having a behavior meltdown. Giving in to this behavior teaches children that impatience pays off. Instead, a calm but firm explanation teaches children that they can't always get what they want when they want it.
7. *Do reward patience.* Try to always acknowledge your child's patient behavior. In the end, children who learn patience can also overcome adversity in healthy, productive ways, says Dr. Benoit.

## *11 Ways to Help Your Child Be Self-Confident*

1. *Practice attachment parenting.* Building self-confidence begins in infancy. A high-touch style of parenting induces self-worth; the baby feels worth and likes it.
2. *Be a positive mirror.* Preschoolers learn about themselves through their parent's reactions. If you react in a positive way to what she does, she will feel valued. Does she feel she

is fun to be with? Does he think that his behavior pleases you?

3. *Play with your child.* Children learn through play. Get your mind off of work and focus your attention on play. It will make your child feel important.

4. *Call your child by his or her name.* Learn to associate the use of your child's name with the message you are giving. For instance, "Hi, Suzy" is a relaxed greeting, while "Jonathon, come here this minute" signals a serious matter.

5. *Be aware of the carry-over principle.* A child who enjoys a school activity receives a boost to his self-worth that carries over to other activities, and as schoolwork improves, his overall self-confidence will grow.

6. *Set your child up to succeed.* Encourage your child's abilities and skills. Support her efforts to develop new skills, and don't expect her to excel just because you did.

7. *Screen your child's friends.* Relatives, coaches, teachers, and friends affect the values and self-worth of your child. Screen out the bad influences and look for positive ones. Encourage those that will help to build your child's character.

8. *Eliminate labels.* Any kind of label—ADHD, gifted, diabetic, or picky eater—focuses on that label and not the child. Concentrate on the whole individual.

9. *Monitor school influences on your child.* Ground your child in a firm value system to guide him as he comes in contact with other values.

10. *Give your child responsibilities.* Create job charts listing jobs to be done. Let your child choose, and rotate the jobs. Divide them into paying extra credit jobs and nonpaying or expected ones.

11. *Encourage your child to express feelings.* This doesn't mean your child should fire away or explode every time she feels like it. Help your child develop a balance between expressing and controlling feelings.[3]

## 13 Ways to Develop Independence

### Preschool

1. Don't overreact when your toddler says no. He is trying to assert his independence. Be certain that discipline is necessary before you administer it.
2. Offer your child choices. For example, ask, "Which cookie do you want?"
3. Don't confine your toddler. Instead allow him to explore new territory.
4. Remember that striving to be independent is part of your child's normal development.

### Primary Grades

5. When your child makes a decision, insist that he stick by it.
6. Let your child express his ideas. Don't belittle them.
7. Let your child plan short family trips.
8. Encourage her to look for alternate ways of doing things.
9. Teach your child to think of more than one way to solve a problem. Do they work?

### Upper Grades

10. Increase the amount of responsibility that you give your child.
11. Develop a sense of trust. Don't ask for every detail of his daily schedule.
12. Support your child when he wants to do something out of the ordinary.
13. Talk about stories in which the main character refused to conform.

## Sharpen Your Child's Decision-Making Skills

1. *Don't overpower your youngster with too many choices.* Limit your child's options to a couple, such as, "What color of socks would you like to wear—the red or the blue ones?"

2. *Only offer choices that you can live with.* Don't say, "What would you like to wear?" unless you are willing to live with a hodgepodge of colors and designs including polka dots, stripes that don't match, and clothes that are not appropriate for the occasion.

3. *Allow for the natural consequences of your child's behavior.* Allow your child to make decisions—even bad ones—on his own. For instance, if your child is a picky eater and he decides he doesn't want to eat lunch, live with it. But don't give in when he whines that he is hungry an hour or two later.

4. *Don't overreact to wrong decisions.* If your child purposely draws on the wall or furniture with her crayons, put the crayons away and let her help you clean up the mess. Say, "Since you used the crayons inappropriately, you won't be able to color any more today."

5. *Make appropriate decisions.* Decisions about right and wrong and health and safety are yours alone to make. You decide when you must hold your child's hand, when to wear a hat, and when it's too cold to go outdoors. State the rule and don't give in.[4]

## 12 Ways to Show Your Child Respect

Do you want your child to show respect? Experts say that children who experience respect are more likely to show it. And parents have the most influence on how respectful children become. If a child is disrespectful at home, chances are the child's disrespect will show up in other situations. When a child experiences respect, he or she knows what it feels like and begins to understand how important it is, experts say. Here are some ways to show your child respect:

1. *Be honest.* Admit when you are wrong and apologize; expect your child to be totally honest.

174

2. *Be positive.* Insults and making fun of your child have no place in your relationship. Compliment good, respectful behavior.

3. *Show trust.* Accept your child's choices and his or her responsibility for these choices.

4. *Be fair in the way you treat your child.* If there is a problem, listen to both sides of the story before reaching a conclusion.

5. *Be courteous.* Most of the time "please," "thank you," and "I'm sorry" will get you the response you want to hear. Remember to knock before you enter your child's room.

6. *Be dependable.* Keep your promises, and show your child that you mean what you say.

7. *Listen to your child.* Take a few minutes to sit down and be an attentive listener. You may be surprised to hear what your child has to say.

8. *Explain why a rule is important.* For instance, if 4:00 to 6:00 is "no TV time," explain that you want your child to concentrate on homework without interruptions.

9. *Highlight self-respect.* When children respect themselves, it's easier for them to respect others.

10. *Believe in your child.* Your opinion counts. Knowing that his parents believe in him is a powerful motivation for a child to succeed.

11. *Help your child set goals for success.* When goals are achieved, self-respect soars.

12. *Show love.* Kids thrive on hugs and kisses. Don't be ashamed to say "I love you." When your child makes a mistake, remind her that you still love her.

## Teach Honesty and Responsibility

Honesty and responsibility are values that take time and patience for your child to truly absorb. Don't be alarmed if you have to stress them time and time again. Letting your child explain what's on his mind shouldn't be frightening if it is handled the right way. To get your child to tell the truth, try the following suggestions.

1. Teach your child that he or she can be honest without you getting upset or yelling.
2. Avoid confrontations in which fibbing is made easy for your children. If you catch Kathy red-handed coloring the wall with crayons, don't ask, "Did you color on the wall?" It sets your child up for a lie. A better way to quiz her is to say, "Tell me about the colored wall."
3. Be honest yourself, and don't ever lie to your children. They will figure it out and decide that telling a lie is okay.
4. Be careful of unintentional lies, such as "I'll be there in a minute," when you don't follow through.
5. Be careful of "white lies" (see below).

| White Lies | The Truth |
| --- | --- |
| It's not medicine; it tastes good. | It tastes like motor oil. |
| This won't hurt. | It feels like a form of torture. |
| I have to buy one thing at the store. | You load the SUV with purchases. |
| It will just be a few minutes. | It seems like forever. |

Instead of a white lie, the honest statement might be something like this:

1. For a dose of yucky medicine, say, "This medicine will make you feel better."
2. Try not to talk about pain, but if you must, say, "This may not feel so good."
3. Planning to go to the grocery store? Say, "I have some shopping to do, and I don't know how long I'll be."
4. If you're planning a short trip, say, "We're going to your aunt's house, and we'll come home at 11:30."

## Books That Teach Values

1. *The Case of the Double Cross* (I Can Read Book 2) by Crosby Bonsall (Harper Trophy, 1982). 64 pages. Reading level: baby to preschool. The book's theme is fairness. The boys don't want any girls in their clubhouse, but a funny little man double-crosses them with a message in code. Then Marigold and her girlfriends get to show just how the boys need them.
2. *The Two of Them* by Aliki (Harper Trophy, 1987). 32 pages. Reading level: ages 4–8. The theme is trust. "The day she was born, her grandfather made her a ring of silver and a polished stone, because he loved her already." And when he became sick, she took care of him with as much love as he had always shown her. *The Two of Them* is a touching story of the respect and love shared by a grandfather and his granddaughter.
3. *The Grouchy Ladybug* by Eric Carle (Harper Trophy, 1996). 48 pages. Reading level: ages 4–8. The theme is respect. A grouchy ladybug is looking for a fight, and she challenges everyone she meets, regardless of their size or strength. The animals she challenges get bigger and bigger until she gets some sense knocked in her head by a whale and becomes a nicer, happier, better-behaved bug.
4. *The Velveteen Rabbit* by Margery Williams (first published in 1922; Avon Reissue, 1999). 33 pages. Reading level: ages 4–8. The book's theme is love. This is a great read-aloud for all ages, or children 8 years and up can read it on their own. A stuffed toy rabbit (with real thread whiskers) comes to life in Margery Williams's timeless tale of love. The Velveteen Rabbit, a Christmas gift to a young boy, lives in the nursery with the other toys hoping to be chosen as a playmate. The Velveteen Rabbit learns from the wise Skin Horse that when a child really, really loves a toy, it becomes Real.
5. *Tinker's Christmas* by Sandra Jones Cropsey (C Works, 2002). 64 pages. Reading level: ages 4–8. Beautifully

illustrated, *Tinker's Christmas* is a fairy tale that teaches respect. Tinker, a young elf, is shy, clumsy, and often taunted and teased by the other elves. He is a flop at the jobs given him until he is assigned the job of Chief Mechanic of the Village Express. When the reindeer come down with the chicken pox a week before Christmas, Santa turns to Tinker to find another way to deliver the toys.

6. *Nothing's Fair in Fifth Grade* by Barthe De Clements (Puffin, 1990). 144 pages. Reading level: ages 8–12. The book teaches respect. The story is a winner of thirteen state "children's favorite" awards. Jenny is certain that the new fat girl is the thief who steals people's lunch money to buy candy. But when the class finds out that the new girl has serious home problems, they learn to accept her.

7. *Ida Early Comes over the Mountain* by Robert Burch (Peter Smith Publishing, 2001). 145 pages. Reading level: ages 9–12. The book's theme is caring. The Amazon book review tells the reader how "tough times in rural Georgia during the Depression take a lively turn when spirited Ida Early arrives to keep house for the Suttons."

8. *Pearl's Promise* by Frank Asch (Yearling, reprint edition 1994). 152 pages. Reading level: ages 9–12. The theme is responsibility. Your kids will love Pearl, a mouse who promised to look after her little brother in a pet store. But she watches with horror as he is chosen to be a snake's next meal. Luckily, the snake's stomach is full and Pearl has time to save him! This is a true winner, well-written and full of adventure.

9. *Summer of the Swans* by Betsy Byars (Puffin, 2005). 144 pages. Reading level: ages 9–12. A winner of the Newbery Medal. The book's theme is responsibility. Fourteen-year-old Sara's life has always flowed smoothly, but this summer is turning out to be a confusing time in her life. Like a swan she wants to fly away from everything: her beautiful older sister, her bossy aunt, her remote father. But most of all she wants to fly away from herself, until her mentally

handicapped little brother Charlie disappears and she is forced to see her life in a new way.

10. *My Brother Sam Is Dead* by James Lincoln Collier (Scholastic, 2005). 224 pages. Reading level: ages 12 and up. The story emphasizes the value of trust. Tragedy strikes the Meeker family during the American Revolution when one son joins the rebel forces and the rest of the family tries to stay neutral in a town loyal to the British crown.

Additional books that teach values:

| Title | Author | Reading Level | Theme | Pages |
|---|---|---|---|---|
| *Clancy's Coat* | Eva Bunting | Ages 4–6 | Respect | 48 |
| *The Berenstain Bears and the Truth* | Stan Berenstain | Ages 4–8 | Truthfulness | 32 |
| *Listening to the Mukies* | Robert Bohlken | Ages 4–8 | Respect and fairness | 104 |
| *The Cat Ate My Gymsuit* | Paula Danziger | Ages 9–12 | Respect | 141 |
| *Thank You, Jackie Robinson* | Barbara Cohen | Teen fiction | Fairness | 128 |

# 13

# Create an Action Plan for School Success

In this chapter you will find action plans important to your child's school success. An effective way to use these ideas is to create a plan of action and start small. Read through this chapter to find one or two techniques you can use to help your child's school performance, and then turn to the appropriate chapter for more help. When you are satisfied with the progress your child makes in one area, try other techniques. Remember, you don't need to read *The ABCs of School Success* from cover to cover. Instead, keep your copy handy; dive in and find the information you need.

## A Preschool Action Plan

*5 Ways to Build Your Preschooler's Enthusiasm for Learning*

1. Use the TV as a teaching station. Check the schedule for educational programs. Set a limit on other programs your child watches.

2. Talk about interesting subjects. Discuss topics new to your child.
3. Have a good selection of children's books at home. Make regular trips to the public library.
4. Set a time each day for reading to your children.
5. Plan daily excursions and talk over your experiences.

## 10 Tips to Help You Pick a Preschool

Choosing a preschool means being picky and asking a lot of questions. Don't wait too long to find a preschool for your child. Begin your search several months before your child is scheduled to begin school.

1. Find a licensed preschool with a good reputation. Look for a school that is known for its friendly atmosphere.
2. Don't hesitate to ask for the names and numbers of parents who have children enrolled in the school, and check out their opinions of the preschool.
3. Always base your judgment on what you see happening at the school.
4. Look for flexibility. For instance, a prospective school should allow some flexibility in pick-up and drop-off times, but it also should have established, written regulations.
5. Look for a school that encourages parents to drop in unannounced and involves you in school activities such as school field trips.
6. Ask about the school's curriculum. A good preschool's daily schedule will include time for individual activities, socializing, crafts, meals and snacks, and free time. Watching TV and videos should not play a major part in the school day.
7. Does the curriculum change over time, offering your child opportunities to learn new concepts?
8. Is the staff qualified? Preschool teachers should have at least two years of college and a background in early childhood development.

9. Does the school's philosophy about sleep, eating, and discipline match yours?
10. Look for facilities that are clean and safe. Look at the floors, eating area, kitchen, bathrooms, and outside play area for dirty or unsafe equipment.

## Build Your Preschooler's Social and Emotional Development

Preschool children start school with different degrees of social and emotional maturity. These qualities take time and practice to develop. Give your child opportunities at home to begin to develop the following positive qualities.

1. *Confidence.* Preschool children must feel good about themselves and believe they can succeed. Confident kids are more willing to attempt new tasks and to try again if they don't succeed the first time.
2. *Independence.* Children must learn to do things for themselves.
3. *Motivation.* Children must want to learn.
4. *Curiosity.* Children show natural curiosity about new things.
5. *Persistence.* Your preschool child should learn to finish what she starts.
6. *Cooperation.* Does he get along, share, and take turns with his playmates?
7. *Self-control.* Does she play without hitting, biting, or other unacceptable behavior?
8. *Empathy.* He is beginning to have an interest in others and understand how others feel.

## Start Now to Develop Your Child's Language

Long before your child enters school, you can help her develop language skills. Here's how:

1. *Begin at birth to talk to your child.* Voices from a television or radio don't have the same effect as a parent who responds to a baby's coos and babbles.
2. *Respond to your baby's language.* Your child will learn that when he makes a certain sound—for example, "mama, mama, mama," you will respond with a smile and talk to him. The more you talk to your baby, the more he will learn and the more he will have to talk about as he gets older.
3. *Give your child opportunities to play.* Through play children explore, become creative, develop social skills, and learn to solve problems.
4. *Guide your child as she learns new activities.* If your preschool child is unable to put a puzzle together, point to a piece and say, "I think this is the piece we need for this space. Why don't you try it?" Then have her pick up the piece and place it in the puzzle. As your child becomes more familiar with how the pieces fit into the puzzle, gradually withdraw your support.
5. *Listen to your child.* Listening is the best way to learn what's on her mind and to discover what she knows and doesn't know. It also shows your child that her feelings and thoughts are valuable.[1]

## An Elementary School Action Plan

### Is Kindergarten Too Much for Your Child?

Early childhood experts know that for children between the ages of five and seven, social and emotional development are as important as learning their ABCs. Furthermore, testing before the third grade gives only a hint of later performance. And children have different learning styles, calling for a whole-child approach. The current emphasis on tests and test results and the pressures on five-year-old children to learn more words and more math problems are often too much for children. Here are seven ways to tell if kindergarten is too much too soon:

1. School administrators favor a rigid academic curriculum rather than a child-friendly style.
2. Your five-year-old child is distraught over homework that includes writing a story. She cries because she can't do it.
3. During a class visit, you see your child fall asleep at her desk.
4. Music, dance, art, physical education, social studies, and science take a backseat to reading and math.
5. You believe that your child's early school experience is being spoiled by an emphasis on high-stakes testing to see if each child is hitting the school and state achievement goals.
6. You're worried that too many tests in kindergarten will give your child a taste of failure before he learns to tie his shoes.
7. You think that if he doesn't do well on the tests, he may have to repeat the grade or attend mandatory summer school.

### Build Your Elementary School Child's Language

Share conversations with your child at meals and other times you are together. Children learn words more easily when they hear them spoken often. Introduce new and interesting words at every opportunity. Here's how:

1. *Be a reader and a writer.* Children learn habits from the people around them.
2. *Read together every day.* Spend time talking about stories, pictures, and words.
3. *Reread familiar books.* Children need practice in reading comfortably and with expression using books they know.
4. *Be your child's best advocate.* Keep informed about your child's progress in reading, and ask the teacher about ways you can help.

185

5. *Visit the library often.* Story times, computers, homework help, and other exciting activities await the entire family.
6. *Build reading accuracy.* As your child is reading aloud, point out words he missed and help him read words correctly. If you stop to focus on a word, have your child reread the whole sentence to be sure he understands the meaning.
7. *Build reading comprehension.* Talk with your child about what she is reading. Ask about new words. Talk about what happened in a story. Ask about the characters, places, and events that took place. Ask what new information she has learned from the book. Encourage her to read on her own.

For a listing of read-aloud stories and books for older children, turn to chapter 1 and chapter 12. Begin with the read-aloud classic *The Velveteen Rabbit,* a tale about a toy rabbit that comes to life. And for older children, start with *Nothing's Fair in Fifth Grade,* a book that teaches respect. And don't forget the math stories: *Money Monster* and *Counting on Frank.*

For a list of books that develop emotional intelligence, turn to chapter 3.

### Identify How Your Child Learns

Children generally fit into one of the following four styles of learning. Determine your child's learning style and, if necessary, adjust his educational program to match those needs.

1. *Spatial/visual children* learn by visualizing images. They can read and understand complex maps, charts, and diagrams, and they are fascinated by machines and inventions.
2. The *kinetic learner* is a child who communicates through body language and gestures. She would rather show than

186

tell you about something, and she enjoys scary amusement rides. She is naturally athletic.

3. A *language oriented* youngster usually reads well and spells words accurately and easily. He remembers names, dates, and trivia, and he likes to play word games.

4. The *logical* child computes math problems quickly in his head. His favorite pastimes are puzzles and strategy games. He likes to figure out how things work, and he constantly asks questions.

## An Action Plan for Creative Development

Make copies of the following brainstorming rules and discovery checklist, and use them for family problem-solving sessions and to jump-start new ideas.

### Brainstorming Rules

1. Free your imagination.
2. Wait to judge the ideas.
3. The more ideas the better.
4. Combine your ideas to make them better.

### Discovery Checklist

| Discovery Questions | What Happens? |
| --- | --- |
| 1. Can I take part of it away? | |
| 2. Can I change its color? | |
| 3. Can I find another use for it? | |
| 4. Can I multiply or divide it? | |
| 5. Can I make it smaller or larger? | |
| 6. Can I take it apart? | |
| 7. Can I change its position? | |
| 8. Can I give it light? | |
| 9. Can I give it touch or texture? | |
| 10. Can I give it motion or sound? | |

For more information about your child's creative abilities, refer to chapter 3, "Learning and Creativity."

## An Action Plan for Problem Behavior

Mental health professionals agree that feeling sad or blue once in a while is a normal part of a child's life. But blues that last for more than a couple of weeks may signal serious depression. Use the following questions to help you evaluate your child's moods and behavior. Circle yes or no for each question.

| | | |
|---|---|---|
| 1. Has your child stopped enjoying nearly all activities? | Yes | No |
| 2. Does your child appear sad? | Yes | No |
| 3. Does she constantly complain of being tired? | Yes | No |
| 4. Does he cry for long periods but can't explain his tears? | Yes | No |
| 5. Does he often become agitated or angry, or does she mask her depression with displays of anger? | Yes | No |
| 6. Have you noticed a change in your child's eating habits? | Yes | No |
| 7. Have you observed a significant weight loss or gain? | Yes | No |
| 8. Do you worry about your child's sleeping habits? | Yes | No |
| 9. Does your child complain about sleepless nights? | Yes | No |
| 10. Does he or she sleep excessively? | Yes | No |
| 11. Is your child's thinking slow, confused, and indecisive? | Yes | No |
| 12. Does your child feel worthless? | Yes | No |
| 13. Does she blame herself excessively? | Yes | No |
| 14. Does he feel inappropriate guilt? | Yes | No |
| 15. Does she talk about death and suicide or has she attempted suicide? | Yes | No |

If you answered yes to question 15 or to the majority of questions, get immediate help. Call your local police or the National Suicide Hot Line (1-800-784-2433).

If you would like to review more information about childhood depression and its symptoms, turn to chapter 6, "Recognizing Problems."

## An Action Plan for a Child Who Fears School

### Pinpointing Your Child's Fear

Kids sometimes have difficulty pinpointing and expressing fears. Here are some fears children of various ages experience as reported by mothers, psychologists, and teachers. Use the following list of fears as a guide to help you determine why your child is afraid to attend school.

1. Afraid someone will beat her up at the bus stop or on the school yard
2. Teasing from peers about personal appearance or learning problems
3. Being ignored by peers
4. High expectations and too much homework
5. A change of schools and teachers
6. Fears being late for the school bus
7. Separation anxiety
8. Multiple teachers and classes scare him

### What Children Might Say If They Are Being Bullied

1. I don't know what happened; I just fell down.
2. My stomach aches; I have a headache; I think I'm going to throw up.
3. I can't go to sleep; I'll have bad dreams.
4. I don't know what happened to my backpack; I guess I just lost it.
5. I don't like school; I wish I could quit.
6. I'm in a special education class, and the other kids make fun of me.

For more on bullies and how they treat their victims, turn to chapter 4, "Home and School Safety."

189

## An Action Plan for Your Special Education Child

If you believe that your child may need special education placement, understanding the placement process is essential. The following true-false statements will help you understand the complex federal laws regulating special education. The correct answer follows each statement.

1. **Statement:** The law is not specific about the parental rights of special education children.
   **Answer:** False. You must be fully informed about all of the rights provided to you and your child under the law.
2. **Statement:** There is no guarantee that tuition will not be charged.
   **Answer:** False. A free, public education for all children is required.
3. **Statement:** You may request an evaluation if you think your child needs special education or related services.
   **Answer:** True. It is your right as a parent to request an educational evaluation if you believe your child needs special education services.
4. **Statement:** You will be notified if the school wishes to evaluate your child.
   **Answer:** True. Your permission is required for all special education services.
5. **Statement:** Your consent for placement is not required by law.
   **Answer:** False. Your permission is required for all special education services. You have the right to appeal the conclusions and determination. The school is required to provide you with information about how to make an appeal.
6. **Statement:** Your child's educational program will be reviewed only if you request a review.
   **Answer:** False. It must be reviewed at least once during each calendar year, and the school must reevaluate your child at least once every three years. If you think your child's current

190

educational placement is no longer appropriate, ask for a reevaluation.

7. **Statement:** All evaluations should be completed in English, even if it is not the child's native language.

   **Answer:** False. You may have your child tested in the language he or she knows best.

8. **Statement:** You may review all of your child's records and obtain free copies of these records.

   **Answer:** True. If the information in your child's records is inaccurate or misleading or violates the privacy or other rights of your child, you may ask that the information be changed. If the school refuses your request, you have the right to a hearing, and if that demand is refused, you may file a complaint with your state educational agency.

9. **Statement:** You may participate in the development of your child's Individualized Education Program (IEP).

   **Answer:** True. The school must make every possible effort to arrange the meeting at a time and place that is convenient for both you and the school. You may participate in the decisions including your child's placement.

10. **Statement:** The school should make every effort to develop an educational program appropriate for your child.

    **Answer:** True. The school will provide your child with the services and support needed in order to be taught with children who do not have disabilities.

11. **Statement:** You may request a due process hearing or voluntary mediation to resolve differences with the school that can't be resolved informally.

    **Answer:** True. Make your request in writing, date your request, and keep a copy for your records.

12. **Statement:** You should be kept informed about your child's progress at least as often as parents of children who do not have disabilities.

    **Answer:** True. Try to schedule regular conferences with your child's special education teacher.

Review chapter 8 for additional information about ADHD children. For detailed information about special education programs, review chapter 9.

## Getting Involved in Your Child's Education

As a psychologist and teacher, I know that parent involvement is a key to school success. Here are a few ways you can get involved in your child's education:

1. Highlight reading. Read aloud and discuss a wide variety of topics with your child.
2. Occasionally stop by your child's classroom to say hello and to ask how he or she is doing.
3. Observe your child's classroom behavior and discuss it with the teacher.
4. Ask for a referral and testing if you think your child would benefit from a special class placement.
5. Volunteer to be a classroom tutor for the kids who need special help.
6. Volunteer to go on a class or school field trip.
7. Bring cookies or special treats to a class party.

For more information on how parents can help to make good schools, turn to chapter 10.

## The Pros and Cons of Homeschooling

### Advantages of Homeschooling Your Child

1. Homeschooled children avoid inappropriate peer pressure.
2. Home education promotes good communication and emotional closeness between family members.
3. It develops a positive home influence and parental involvement.

4. Education may be tailored to the child's learning style, interests, and pace.
5. Family values are strengthened.

## Disadvantages of Homeschooling Your Child

1. Parents must be prepared to spend all day with their children.
2. Parents must supervise lessons, check progress, think of activities, and make worksheets.
3. Twenty-four hours a day with children plus being their teacher is no joke.
4. Materials are expensive, so home education isn't cheaper than public school education.
5. You may need to quit your job to be a full-time homeschool teacher.
6. Even if you are not in the mood, you have to appear enthusiastic about the material you are teaching.

Refer to chapter 11 for additional information on homeschooling and distance learning.

## An Action Plan for Teaching Values and Rules

### Ways to Instill Values

1. Talk about the moral dilemmas you faced in childhood and how you handled them. Try it at bedtime; your kids will love it.
2. Follow your own values to the letter. Your kids will learn values by imitating you, and that's scary.
3. Be a positive example of what you believe.
4. Pay attention to the values your child might learn from others. Who does she try to imitate?
5. Ask questions that will lead to a discussion of values.
6. Don't preach to your child after he or she has messed up. Try to relax and wait until you can talk calmly.

7. Limit your child's exposure to video games and TV. If you limit your own TV time, it will suggest that there are more valuable ways for your child to spend his or her time.
8. Encourage your children to help others. Be generous with your time and money, and your child will learn to donate money and time to important causes.
9. Have frequent conversations about values, and let your kids hear about what you believe.
10. Have high expectations. Expect your children to reflect positive values.

## Steps to Smart Family Rules

If rules are a problem in your family, try the following suggestions.

1. Brainstorm the problem. Explain that all comments are welcome and you are not to criticize each other's ideas.
2. Divide a sheet of notebook paper into two columns.
3. In the first column, list important family values. Do you want your child to develop self-control? To tell the truth? To value hard work?
4. In the second column, write your family rules. You might want your children to come home on time, show proper table manners, bathe regularly, and wear clean clothes.
5. Try to link your family rules to your values. Eliminate unnecessary or imprecise rules.
6. Agree with your child on a final list of values and family rules.

To review additional information about teaching your child important values and rules, return to chapter 12.

# A Final Word

One of my grandchildren was in trouble almost from the day he stepped into a first-grade classroom. His behavior was atrocious; he hit his classmates, ran away during recess, and refused to do his assignments. He was in the lowest reading group, and it looked like his education would turn out to be a disaster. I was alarmed and saddened by his school behavior, because it just didn't match the loving and obedient child I saw at home with his family.

His parents were alarmed too, but with the help of regular parent-teacher conferences, his school behavior and achievement improved. His teacher helped to develop a reward system that included firm discipline and an emphasis on appropriate behavior and school achievement. Gradually his behavior improved. Now as he is going into high school, his grades are good, he loves to read, he enjoys extracurricular activities, and he likes school.

Preparing your child for a successful school experience is a difficult and challenging task—one that requires good parenting but not perfect parents. Review the lists, tips, and strategies in *The ABCs of School Success* for essential information to help your child succeed. Finally, be an example of the attitudes and behavior you want your child to imitate, and you certainly will make a difference in your child's school performance.

# Notes

### Chapter 1: Make Learning Fun

1. Melissa Hendricks, "The Origins of Babble," *Johns Hopkins Magazine*, February 1988, available online at http://www.jhu.edu/~jhumag/0298web/baby.html.

2. Dimitri Christakis, quoted in Sheryl Ubelacker, "Too Many Kids Under 2 Watching TV," CNEWS, May 7, 2007, http://cnews.canoe.ca/CNEWS/Canada/2007/05/07/4161126-cp.html.

3. Mary C. Rose, "Don't Stop Now—Reading Aloud to Children," *Instructor*, May-June 1999, 8.

4. Jane Braunger, "In the Beginning," *NW Education*, Fall 1998, 15.

5. "Why We Love Picture Books," *Parade*, September 22, 2002.

6. Ellen Nathan, Director and Language Arts Specialist for the Screen Actors Guild Book PALS program, http://www.bookpals.net/index.php.

### Chapter 2: Growing Up Smart

1. Alex Osborne, *Applied Imagination* (New York: Charles Scribner's Sons, 1963), 165.

2. See "Boys at School: A National Crisis," Family Education, http://school.familyeducation.com/gender-studies/school-psychology/38493.html.

3. "Intelligence in Men and Women Is a Gray and White Matter," *Today@UCI*, January 20, 2005. Dr. Michael T. Alkire, Kevin Head of UCI, and Ronald A. Yeo of New Mexico University participated in the

197

2005 study supported in part by the National Institute of Child Health and Human Development, http://today.uci.edu/news/release_detail .asp?key=1261.

### Chapter 3: Learning and Creativity

1. Daniel E. Goleman, *Emotional Intelligence: Why It Can Matter More Than IQ* (New York: Bantam Books, 2005), 80–83.
2. Ibid., 80–81.
3. Adapted from Leah Davis, MEd., "Emotional Intelligence: An Essential Compound of Education," *Kelly Bear*, October 2000, http://www .kellybear.com/TeacherArticles/TeacherTip3.html.
4. *Inclusion of Students with Disabilities*, National Association of School Psychologists, a Handout for Teachers, http://www.nasponline .org/communications/spawareness/Inclusion.pdf.
5. Adapted from Wesley Sharpe, *Growing Creative Kids* (Broadman and Holman, 1993), 45–47.
6. Michael LeBoeuf, *Imagineering* (New York: McGraw-Hill, 1980).
7. Adapted from Sharpe, *Growing Creative Kids*, 77–78.
8. Ibid., 120.
9. Tom Mullen, *Laughing Out Loud* (Richman, IN: Friends United Press, 1989), 112.
10. Adapted from Sharpe, *Growing Creative Kids*, 98.
11. Ibid., 103–4.

### Chapter 4: Home and School Safety

1. Adapted from the National Center for Missing and Exploited Children, http://www.missingkids.com.
2. "Personal Safety for Children: A Guide for Parents," The National Center for Missing and Exploited Children, http://www.missingkids .com/en_US/publications/NC122.pdf.
3. Ibid., 9.
4. Wesley Sharpe, "The Left-out Child," *HomeLife* magazine, February 2000, reprinted in Partnership for Learning, http://www.partnershipfor learning.org/article.asp?ArticleID=1646.
5. Jennifer Shroff Pendley, "Bullying and Your Child," © 2005 Encylopaedia Britannica, Inc. and www.kidshealth.org, quote found on http:// mobbingopinion.bpweb.net/artman/publish/article_1610.shtml.
6. *USA Weekend*, April 2000.
7. "Unicel Takes a Stand Against Cyber Bullying," Unicel Press Release, September 14, 2006, available online at CSR Wire, http://www.csrwire .com/News/6334.

8. Rosalind Wiseman, "How to Fight the New Bullies," *Parade*, February 25, 2007, 8.

9. Ibid., 6.

10. Ibid.

## Chapter 5: Effective Discipline

1. Virginia M. Shiller, *Rewards for Kids! Ready-to-Use Charts and Activities for Positive Parenting* (Washington, DC: American Psychological Association, 2003).

2. Dr. Scott Turansky and Joanne Miller, *Parenting Is Heart Work*, audiotape series, National Center for Biblical Parenting.

3. John Krumboltz, *Changing Children's Behavior* (Upper Saddle River, NJ: Prentice-Hall, 1972), 3.

4. "Teaching Young Children Self-Control Skills" (Bethesda, MD: National Association of Schools, 2002), http://www.nasponline.org/resources/handouts/behavior%20template.pdf.

## Chapter 6: Recognizing Problems

1. Adapted from "Developing Your Child's Self-Esteem," Kids Health, 2005, http://www.kidshealth.org/parent/emotions/feelings/self_esteem.html.

2. Shelly Wilson, "One on One with Adrienne Johnson," *Gball Online Magazine* © 2000 Momentum Media, http://www.gballmag.com/qa-ajohnson.html.

3. H. Norman Wright, *Helping Your Kids Handle Stress* (San Bernardino, CA: Here's Life Publishers, 1989), 75–80.

4. Judith Becerra, "Kids and Cheating," C. S. Mott Children's Hospital, University of Michigan Health System, 2006, http://www.med.umich.edu/1libr/pa/pa_kidcheat_bhp.htm.

## Chapter 7: School Phobia

1. Laurie Winslow Sargent, "Name that Fear," *Christian Parenting Today*, November/December 1991, 51.

2. Robert Spitzer, MD, *Diagnostic and Statistical Manual of Mental Disorders*, rev. ed. (Washington, DC: American Psychiatric Press, 1989), 299, 351.

3. Maureen Hogan, PhD, "School Phobia," *Nassau County Psychologist*, http://www.fenichel.com/Current.shtml.

4. Caroline Clauss, "When Going Back to School Is Not Going On Children Speak Out: Shyness and School Phobia," *New York City*

*Voices,* September/October 1999, http://www.nycvoices.org/article.php?author_id=&article_id=114.

5. Wesley Sharpe, "School Phobia," *Christian Parenting Today,* November/December 1991, 48–55.

## Chapter 8: Take Charge of Your ADHD Child

1. Rebecca Kajander, *A Parent's View of ADHD* (Minneapolis: Park Nicollet Medical Foundation, 1995), 34.

2. Russell A. Barkley, PhD, *Taking Charge of ADHD* (New York: The Guilford Press, 1995), 73.

3. Ibid., 69.

4. Ibid.

5. Ibid., 105.

6. Ibid., 106.

7. Elaine McEwan, EdD, *Attention Deficit Disorder* (Wheaton, IL: Harold Shaw Publishers, 1995), 6.

8. Ibid., 92.

9. Ibid., 35.

## Chapter 9: All about Special Education

1. Wesley Sharpe, "Special Education Inclusion: Making It Work," Education World, 2005, http://www.educationworld.com/a_curr/curr320.shtml.

2. "What Is Impairment, Disability, or Handicapping Condition?" School District of River Falls Special Education, April 18, 2006, http://www.rfsd.k12.wi.us/departments/special_education/impairmentcondition.htm.

3. Individuals with Disabilities Education Act, IDEA 1997, 2004, http://idea.ed.gov.

4. "How Inclusion Works at White Elementary," University of Kansas Circle of Inclusion Project, 2002, http://circleofinclusion.org/english/demo/wichitawhite/how/index.html.

5. Bill Henderson, "Champions of Inclusion," http://www.inclusive-schools.org/PDF/Champions.pdf.

## Chapter 10: How Good Families Make Good Schools

1. California State Board of Education Policy 89–01, adopted 1989 and revised 1994, http://www.cde.ca.gov/be/ms/po/policy #89-01-sep1994.asp.

2. Lyric Winik, "Good Schools *Can* Happen," *Parade,* August 27, 2006.

3. Ibid.
4. Ibid.
5. Ibid.
6. Roberta Furger, "Making Connections Between Home and School," The George Lucas Educational Foundation, September 16, 2002, http://www.edutopia.org/making-connections-between-home-and-school.
7. "Parent Teacher Conferences," Farnham Elementary School, San Jose, California, 1987, http://www.cambrian.k12.ca.us/farnham/parents/parents_conferences.htm.
8. Winik, "Good Schools *Can* Happen."

**Chapter 11: Success through Homeschooling**

1. Patricia M. Lines, "Homeschooling," *ERIC Digest*, September 2001, http://www.eric.ed.gov/ERICDocs/data/ericdocs2sql/content_storage_01/0000019b/80/19/49/48.pdf.
2. Ibid.
3. "Homeschooling in the United States: 2003," National Center for Educational Statistics, http://nces.ed.gov/pubs2006/homeschool/distancelearning.asp.
4. U.S. Department of Education, http://www.ed.gov/about/offices/list/oii/nonpublic/statistics.html.
5. Seema Mehta, "More Students Across the US Logging on to Online Classrooms," *Los Angeles Times*, February 18, 2007.
6. "Social Skills and Homeschooling: Myths and Facts," http://www.familyeducation.com/article/0,1120,58-17910,00.htm.
7. "About Calvert," Calvert School, http://www.calvertschool.org/education-services.
8. http://www.k12.com.
9. http://www.k12.com/dg/dg_K12_2007.html?se-Google&campaign=National_K12_Brand_Job_926%adgroup=K12_Nat_Brand&k12%20com&gaclid=CMC-nfC4kpACFREplgod8iHx6A.
10. Laurel Springs School website, http://www.laurelsprings.com.
11. "Overview," A Beka Academy, http://www.abekaacademy.org/AcademicPrograms/Overview.html.
12. "Program 1," A Beka Academy, http://www.abekaacademy.org/AcademicPrograms/Program1.html.
13. http://www.sonlight.com/coreultra-packages.html.

**Chapter 12: Don't Forget about Values**

1. Wesley Sharpe, "Plugging the Holes in Your Teens Moral Ozone," in *The Christian Mom's Answer Book* by Mike Yorkey and Sandra P. Aldrich (Colorado Springs: Chariot Victor, 1999), 167.

2. Marilyn Benoit, MD., "The Dot.com Kids and the Demise of Frustration Tolerance," 2005, http://www.allianceforchildhood.org/projects/computers/computers_articles_dot_com_kids.htm.

3. Adapted from Dr. William Sears, "12 Ways to Help Your Child Build Self-Confidence," AskDrSears.com, http://www.askdrsears.com/html/6/T061500.asp.

4. Editors of *Parent* magazine, *The Parents Book of Lists from Birth to Age Three* (New York: St. Martin's Press, 2000), 115.

**Chapter 13: Create an Action Plan for School Success**

1. U.S. Department of Education, "Helping Your Preschool Child," Washington, DC, 2005, http://www.ed.gov/parents/earlychild/ready/preschool/preschool.pdf.

**Wesley Sharpe** (EdD, University of the Pacific) has worked as a public school psychologist, helping to establish programs for children with special needs, including gifted and talented children. He has completed hundreds of psychological and educational evaluations of preschool, elementary, and high school children. Many of the boys and girls he evaluated were emotionally disturbed or learning disabled. Dr. Sharpe is the author of *Growing Creative Kids* and has contributed to *The Christian Mom's Answer Book* and *Lists to Live By*.

# More Resources for Parents

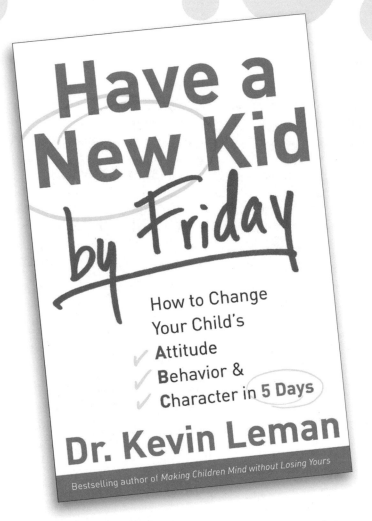

**www.HaveANewKidbyFriday.com**

from **R** Revell

ONE TOUGH
Mother

It's Time
to Step Up
and Be
the Mom

Julie Barnhill

revving up
your marriage
after kids
arrive

date night
*in a*
minivan
lorilee craker

M♥PS